REAL SEX

REAL SEX

BY GRUB SMITH

sex columnist for FHM

HarperCollins*Publishers*

HarperCollins*Publishers*
77–85 Fulham Palace Road,
Hammersmith, London W6 8JB

Published by HarperCollins*Publishers* 1999

9 8 7 6 5 4 3 2 1

A catalogue record for this book is available from
the British Library

ISBN 0 00 257085 8

Set in Garamond and Futura

Design by design principals

Printed and bound in Great Britain by
Scotprint Ltd. Musselburgh

CONTENTS

Acknowledgements

My thanks are due to the many kind people who helped make this book happen.

First of all, a salute to Mike Soutar, Ed Needham, Anthony Noguera, Marcus Rich and Mark Ellen, who collectively came up with the idea that I write a sex column for *FHM*. That their sole motive was a desire to laugh at pictures of my butt in no way detracts from the gratitude I feel.

Similarly right up there on my Christmas card list are Laura Carlile, Regina Wolek, Steve Nash, Susie Pride, Sophie Kenningham and everyone else at *FHM* who put so much work into 'The Laboratory of Love'.

Photographers Neil Cooper, Mick Hutson, Matt Antrobus and Adam Lawrence have taken countless pictures of me naked over the last few years, thus selflessly ruining their chances of ever getting a *Vogue* cover.

My assistant Olivia Quain gave me a lot of 'feminine insights'. Unfortunately, most of them were about cats.

At HarperCollins, I have to thank my editor, Susan Watt, her colleagues Amanda Starkey and Digby Smith, and Jonathan Watt, who came up with the idea in the first place. On the design side of things, my hat goes off to Graham Webb.

I *really* enjoyed working with the naked women who appear in the 'Positions' chapter.

And finally, this book would naturally have been quite impossible without the many whinges and complaints of every girl I've ever slept with.

Especially Annabel.

INTRODUCTION

One of the most shameful things about earning a living as a 'sex expert' is that blonde, curvaceous, attractive teenage women always assume I'm going to be great in bed. As a single man, I naturally do nothing to shatter these illusions, but the truth is I'm pretty mediocre. If the act of sex were to be marked by an international panel of judges, a bit like ice skating, then I can assure you I'd be picking up my fair share of 0.5s. The good news, however, is that I am a lot better at it now than I used to be in my twenties, when — like many young guys — I was a dunce under the duvet.

The turning point came when I was dumped by a girl I really loved. Bad sex wasn't the only factor in our split up, but it was an important one. Realising this in the broken-hearted months that followed — months of sobbing and self-pity, of 1½–litre wine bottles and Willie Nelson records — I decided to bone up on the subject. Never again would my foreplay technique rely on a quick nipple tweak and five minutes of lapping away like a thirsty labrador.

Unfortunately, there was a problem. You see, all the love-making instruction manuals I found in bookshops seemed to be written by stout, matronly agony aunts or by wispy haired, almost certainly vegetarian, men. Sure, they were worthy and well-intentioned, but they placed an undue emphasis on the romance of sex rather than the actual mechanics. Whereas I was

desperately looking for detailed know-how with no pulled punches, these authors preferred to flannel on about 'setting the mood with lemon scented candles' or the joys of an hour-long foot massage. Some of them even believed that horoscopes could influence your performance in bed.

Eventually, I found two volumes which steered clear of this sort of tosh, but even they had their limitations. I can perhaps best demonstrate this with a short quotation from each. First off, we have *The Joy of Sex*. Although admirably upfront, it dates from a period when Vinegar Joe were topping the charts and flared trousers were so wide they could actually be used for shelter on camping holidays. Our society's attitudes on what is and what isn't erotic have moved along fast in the quarter-century since it was published, and I'm afraid to say it shows. Take this gem, for example:

'Women used to chop off their armpit hair, or they did until a new generation realised it was sexy… In fact, armpits should on no account be shaved, as they can be used instead of the palm to silence your partner at climax. If you must use your hand to clasp over his mouth, then make sure you rub it through the aromatic hairs in your own and your partner's armpit area first.'

Needless to say, this sort of behaviour would probably result in a phone call to the police these days, and — for my tastes, anyway — it's a good thing that so few modern women outside of the Bulgarian Discus Academy allow their pits to go troppo. But, that said, it is at least better advice than the wisdom purveyed in my other favourite sex book. Entitled *How to Find and Fascinate a Mistress*, it's one of those butch American bestsellers written by a man so free of self-doubt that you'd bet he'd had an important part of his brain removed. The women in his book are routinely referred to as 'the target' or 'the merchandise', and here he is, at glorious length, on the subtleties of seduction:

'Some men find it difficult to muster a sincere and direct approach with a convincing delivery. If you have this problem, joke your way into the subject. I have found a number of innocent questions which are always revealing and provide an opening for discussion of personal details. One of the most effective is:

'Gee! I wonder how big your boyfriend is.' To this you will always get a smile and some answer: 'Pretty big,' 'He's just a little guy,' 'What boyfriend?' — and that's the one you're waiting for. You don't have to give up on the first two, but it's a lot easier to wait for the last one. Following it up, your next statement is:

'Gee! I find that hard to believe.'

The target just HAS to answer. If not, say it again. Either disappointment or pride will force her to say something to explain her lonely

situation. Regardless of her explanation, your attack must now move to something such as:

'Well look, I don't believe there are enough fools in the world to leave someone like you alone. (Pause. Shake your head twice. Take a deep breath.) I don't want to seem crude, but I'd sure as hell do something about it if I knew you better ...'

Staggering stuff, you'll agree. But even when he focused his undoubted expertise on making love — in such classic chapters as 'The Dribble Problem' or 'Is She Taking Too Long?' — I was left feeling none the wiser.

And, during the years that I've been writing the sex column in *FHM* magazine, I've come to suspect that I'm not the only man looking for answers. I get tons of mail from guys who want genuinely useful details about how to solve their sexual anxieties, rather than the usual flannel to do with 'talking about it' that is commonly dispensed by experts on mid-morning TV shows. That's why I'm writing this book, and maybe it's why you're reading it.[1]

As the title cleverly suggests, this book is about *Real Sex*, and it's for anyone who wants to understand how to be better in bed on a purely physical level. It won't make you love each other any more. It won't shorten the odds that you'll end up living happily ever after together in an ivy-clad cottage. It won't pass on the sensual massage secrets of the mysterious east. But it will make you a better, more capable and adventurous lover.

Like my columns in *FHM*, it's aimed primarily at men. Nevertheless, I daresay it will also prove useful to women, as it provides an insight into what men really want in bed, but haven't been allowed to ask for so loudly since we caved in and gave you the vote. It's not a backlash: it's just concerned with the facts of sex rather than the woolly uncertainties of romance. Women's equality or inequality doesn't come into it — though as I am personally convinced that there's nothing less attractive in bed than a 'new man' asking permission every time he wants to change position, I reckon there's a fair chance that many women will reap the benefits of this book too.

Uniquely for a sex manual, instead of relying on surveys and bland statistics,[2] I have personally tested out everything that's described in here. I have, quite literally, put my arse on the line. I doubt Dr Ruth does this. And, gutsy little veteran though she is, I wouldn't much want to see her do it either. Especially the stuff on page 126.

---

[1] *Although given the 'jokey' photograph on the front cover and the Mr Men sized format, there is admittedly a strong chance that someone bought it for you as an unimaginative last–minute Christmas gift. Still, it's better than socks.*

[2] *Not that all statistics are bland. For instance, I particularly like the fact that 9 per cent of all children growing up on American farms have their first sexual experience with an animal.*

Of course, some people may be offended by the more kinky acts I have recommended, but to these critics I can only say one thing. I used to be like you. I was a meat and potatoes lover who frowned upon (or, more accurately, sniggered at) the antics of sexual perverts. But the more I've learnt about sex, the more I have come to admire these individuals, because they are the ones truly pushing back the boundaries of pleasure. While the rest of us are content to make love routinely in just three or four positions, these pioneers are trying out new, exciting stuff. Sure, some of it is ridiculous, or horrible, or requires dressing up in leather chaps and a World War Two gasmask, but rest assured that I have chosen only those practices which can be tried out by 'normal' couples who have no desire to appear in the *News of the World*. Or court.

Lastly, regular readers may notice that this book, unlike *FHM*, contains no nude pictures of me. What can I say? It's been a good year. I smoke forty Marlboro a day. I am at least two stone overweight. If there *were* photographs of me demonstrating weird positions, it would surely make most sensible adults hurl the book to one side. And I don't want to put people off sex. That would be foolish.

CHAPTER 1 *sex drive*

E ven though I possess the most engaging of prose styles, I realise that you spent at least ten seconds looking at that naked woman before beginning this paragraph. And I don't blame you. I would have done too. Because, as men, we have an imperative to check out all the attractive females we see, making mental notes of their good points and wondering if they might go to bed with us. We can't help it. In fact, we even do it when we're supposed to be concentrating on other, supposedly more important matters, as evidenced by this valuable nugget of data:

Number of men who had car crashes when they drove past those Wonderbra posters featuring Eva Herzigova:	**27**
Number of women who had car crashes when they drove past those Wonderbra posters featuring Eva Herzigova:	**0**

But have you ever wondered why we are made this way? Questioned what useful purpose is served by us being slaves to our libido? Mused upon the fact that even rocket scientists and presidents can be reduced to drooling morons with the decision-making powers of a watermelon if their secretary so much as bends down to fasten her shoe? Well, if you have, then I've got some bad news for you: you're reading the wrong book. You see, I don't *care* about all that deep-seated biological impulse crap, or about how our sexual behaviour was shaped by millions of years of evolution, some of it involving orangutans. All that concerns me is that sex is fun. And discovering new ways to make it even more so.

I'm confident, too, that most men share the same sense of priorities. To judge by the 'agony' letters I receive, they are far more interested in getting laid than the make-up of their chromosomes or the amorous habits of their tree-dwelling forebears. In fact, the most common enquiry I hear is refreshingly straightforward: 'How Can I Make Myself More Attractive to Women?'

The answer? Well, it varies.[1] For every woman who is impressed by the fact that you drive a convertible and know what kind of cheese to buy, they'll be another who thinks you're an insufferable jerk. And the same thing holds true for having large muscles, smoking joints, wearing

[1] *What do you expect for £9.99 — phone numbers?*

designer togs, enjoying fine art, or cultivating enough chest hair to carpet a small apartment. People have different tastes and what it boils down to is this: sure, Brad Pitt is popular, but even Hitler had a girlfriend.

Nevertheless, having spoken to literally tens of women on this subject (a selection of waitresses, journalists, models and stylists who, if I was a younger, blacker man, I might well be tempted to call my 'posse'), I have highlighted a crucial selection of the things that are definitely *not* appealing to the fairer sex. They are:

● **Cheesy chat-up lines:** Face it, girls are onto these. They've heard them all a hundred times.[2] So when you approach a young lady with your so-called witty opener, she's already biting back a yawn of recognition. The consensus of my female survey group was that it's far better to wait for her to look at you, and then hold her gaze for a moment longer than necessary. If she keeps looking as well, this means that she wouldn't mind if you went over and said hi. (Or, admittedly, that you've got something unpleasant coming out of your nose.) Then you just trot over, smile, ask her name and begin a conversation. Which brings us to . . .

● **Talking about yourself:** Naturally, she wants to know something about you, but on a first meeting this should be kept to a bare minimum. A polite 'What do you do, then?' does not mean she will die unless she immediately hears your entire family history, a detailed monologue about the transmission problems of every car you've ever owned, and numerous ill-disguised lies about how much you earn and how many famous people you know. So let the encounter follow the rules of ping-pong, with each of you taking turns. If you can be funny, that's fantastic, but don't avalanche her with gags unless you're prepared to laugh at hers too. As Clive James once wrote, with surprising insight and sensitivity for an Australian, 'People don't want to be charmed, they want to be charming.'

● **Dancing with men:** We've all done this. You're at a nightclub, you and a pal sidle over to some women on the dancefloor, and while you're waiting to pluck up the courage to approach them, you dance with each other. Badly. Now stop for a minute. Think. What does that look like?

Right.

● **Preening yourself:** When I was growing up, the range of grooming products men had to choose from was minuscule. When preparing for a big night out it was basically a case of perming any three from Brylcreem, Blue Stratos, shampoo or soap, and as a result guys would go on the pull displaying all the style and sophistication of mental patients. Thus it is generally considered a good thing that we have smartened ourselves up a bit since then. But one unanimous beef among my panel of young women was that men are now going too far in the opposite direction. 'I hate it when a man never misses a chance to check himself in mirrors,' said one typical correspondent. 'Or when they take even longer to get ready than I do. And I actually chucked one guy I fancied a lot because he used to fold all his clothes up really neatly, even getting the crease in his trousers right, before he'd get into bed with me.

---

[2] And I include 'Hey baby, do you want to play carnival? That's where you sit on my face and I guess your weight.'

You know, I was like "OK, they're expensive, but I'm waiting here, like, *naked*." '

● **Not knowing when you're beaten:** If a woman simply doesn't fancy you, no amount of flowers, poetry or Belgian chocolates is going to win her over. Your best bet is to take it like a man, and hope she stays friendly enough to introduce you to her (possibly just as cute) friends. Ah, but how do you know that she isn't just playing hard to get? Well, again, there seems to be a rule here: if you phone her three times in a week and she doesn't call you back, you've got no chance.

So, if you avoid these blunders you should at least be allowed to keep your dignity, even if you still get the brush-off. But, on the other side of the ledger, is there anything positive men can do? Well, a cursory glance at women's magazines (which very considerately appear to run exactly the same features every month, just in case you missed them before) shows that girls are mostly turned on by stuff like 'a sense of humour', 'a kind personality' and 'nice hands'. This may be true, but it isn't very helpful.[3] Apart from getting a manicure, it's going to be hard for you to shape your sexual destiny.

This sense of helplessness partly explains the continued profits of those companies which promise miracle shortcuts to romantic success, especially the ones flogging pheremones in the back of porno titles. However, while I'm sure most of them are hucksters with a swelling bank account in the Cayman Islands and a vat full of bat urine, they do at least have a point. Smell is an important, if subtle, part of sexual attraction. For example, even if you're no wine connoisseur, you will have noticed that your partner seems to have a different, tangier aroma when she's turned on (especially if you're giving her head at the time), and maybe even that redheads, blondes and brunettes all have their own distinct genital odour. Naturally, the allure of these body smells varies from man to man, and not everyone will respond to their aphrodisiac effects quite as keenly as Napoleon, who used to tell his wife Josephine, 'Don't wash, I'm coming home tonight.' If you're still cynical about this, try a simple, if rather gross, experiment. Next time you're going out to a crowded party, ask your girlfriend to lay off the Obsession and instead dab a little of her 'pussy juice' behind the ears. Then gauge how much more attention she gets than usual.

If you want to harness the power of scent to your own advantage, however, you'd be ill-advised to splash on semen like Brut. Instead, play it straight, and simply make sure your body smells clean and fresh. BO and bad breath may be useful as a temporary expedient for gassing badgers, but they're never going to win fair lady.

---

[3] *And Captain Hook is* fucked.

Fetishes

Thus far, I've been assuming that you're a 'normal' healthy man who fancies 'normal' attractive women. But there's a fair chance that you may have a few kinkier fetishes to boot.[4] These might be as innocent as a fondness for women in black lingerie or as wild as a desire to have stinging insects crawl over your honey-coated scrotum, and you probably feel a little shy about revealing their existence to your partner. But, as it will make your sex life complete if you *can* tell her, it's best to know how and why we develop a fetish in the first place.

Well, most of them get imprinted in our minds during the two main periods of sexual curiosity, which occur from infancy to the age of four, and then later during puberty. Now, while you may not remember having any sexual thoughts in your early years — and personally my recollection of that entire pre-kindergarten era is limited to a) being told off by my dad for throwing stones at the gypsy children, and b) the theme tune to a TV show called '*The Banana Splits*'[5] — you will instantly recognise that your teenage brain divided on roughly the lines of the graph on the left.

And it's because some guys were thinking intensely about sex long before they got a chance to try it out for real, that their desires 'spilled over' onto objects which are merely *associated* with women. Common examples include underwear, nurses' uniforms, schoolgirl outfits, leather gear and spanking, but to demonstrate the general principle, let's just take a look at shoe fetishists. Now you don't have to be Sherlock Holmes to work out that a shoe is the first thing a crawling nipper sees before its mother comes over to pick it up for a cuddle, so it can obviously become linked in the mind with warmth and affection. Also, as high-heeled shoes are designed to alter the posture and spine angle of a woman, emphasising the roundness of the buttocks and the protuberance of the breasts, they may later on become lodged in the adolescent mind as 'arousal triggers'.

Percentage of daily brain activity in males aged 12–16.

Football	6%
Rock music	5%
Picking your nose	3%
Smutty thoughts about girls	86%

---

[4] Possibly even about *boots*.
[5] 'Flippin' like a pancake, poppin' like a cork/ Fleagle, Drooper, Bingo and Snork.'

So far so good. But why do some men take these fancies a little too far? Check out this chap, for instance, who was the subject of a case study in the work of the great Victorian sexologist Richard von Krafft-Ebing:

'Case No. 86. X, a clerk, 50 years old. Appears periodically in brothels and gets involved in conversation with a prostitute. Casting desirous glances at her shoes, he pulls one off then kisses and bites it when weak with desire. Thereupon he thrusts his penis into it until he ejaculates, at which point he rubs the discharge over his chest. Afterwards he begs the owner to let him keep the shoe for a few days, and then returns it with polite thanks after the specified period.'

What's happened here is that he's allowed his fetish to spiral out of control. Instead of just hinting to his lover at home that she looks good in heels, he's become dependent on the shoe itself to get his jollies. It's got so bad that he doesn't even need the prostitute at all. In fact, she's just getting in the way.

Of course, it could be that you yourself have such a full-grown fetish. Perhaps you go through your days pretending to be utterly normal, but under cover of the night give in to your sexual Furies and become . . . Rubberman! Or Torture Boy! Or even the slightly less butch-sounding Bank Manager Who Likes to Wear Nappies and Get Breastfed Person! If so, like X, you may feel a certain amount of shame and embarrassment, and be thinking about getting counselling. My advice would be: don't. If that's what turns you on, just feel the fear and go with it. We live, thank God, in a society which is more and more open to people on the sexual extremes, and the only phone numbers and addresses you'll need are the ones detailed overleaf:

THE SEX ADDRESS BOOK

Many of these groups publish their own newsletter, and will help you link up with fellow enthusiasts in your area. You'll also be able to find plenty more useful contact addresses if you have access to the Internet.

Adult Babies:
Mummy Hazel's Hush-a-bye Baby Club,
c/o 43 South Hill Road, Gravesend, Kent DA12.

Anal sex:
Anal Banal magazine,
c/o 28 Colbery Place, London N16.

Bisexuality:
The Bisexual Resource Centre,
58a Broughton Street, Edinburgh EH1 3SA,
Scotland.

Bondage:
Fantasy of Gord, HG Publications,
PO Box 27, Welshpool SY21 OZZ.

Cybersex:
Future Sex, 60 Federal Street, Suite 502,
San Francisco, CAL 94107, USA.
Tel: 001 415 541 7725.

Exhibitionism:
Steam magazine, PDA Press Ic, Rte 2, Box 1215,
Cazenovia, WI 53924, USA.

Food and 'messy' sex:
Splosh magazine, PO Box 70, St Leonard's on
Sea, East Sussex TN38 OPX.

Foot fetishism:
FFF Society, PO Box 24866, Cleveland,
OH 44124, USA.

Leather:
National Leather Association,
NLA HQ, PO Box 17463,
Seattle, WA 98107, USA.
Tel: 001 206 789 8900.

Piercings:
Metal Morphosis, Peterley Business Centre,
Hackney Road, London E2.

Rubber:
Latex Seduction Club, BP 651, 44018 Nantes,
Cedex 01, France.

S&M:
Fetish Times, BCM Box 9253,
London WC1N 3XX.

Spanking:
The North-East Spanking Society,
c/o TEP PO Box 441,
Waltham, MA 02254-0441, USA.

Swingers:
Desire magazine, 192 Clapham High Street,
London SW4 7UD.
Tel: 0171 627 5155.

Transvestites:
Way Out Tranny Guidebook,
PO Box 941, London SW5 9UT.
Tel: 0181 363 0948.

CHAPTER 2 *preliminaries*

KNOW YOUR BODY

I guess it would be customary in an instructional manual such as this to start off with a scientific description of how your penis works, including sensitive line drawings of stuff like your vas deferens. And, indeed, I am going to do that. But first, let's cut to the chase. Men, except for the lucky few who earn their living by appearing in such masterpieces of garage cinema as *Raiders of the Lost Arse*, worry far more about the size of their cock than its internal workings. In fact, if personal experience is anything to go by, they worry more about the size of their cock than *anything*, and that includes such comparatively footling issues as nuclear war or global warming.

Most women will laugh at such insecurity, claiming that it has more to do with our fear of measuring up to others guys in the locker room than it has to do with sex. They'll tell you that 'size doesn't matter'. They will be caring, considerate and reasonable. Unfortunately, they will also be lying. Indeed, if you were to eavesdrop on these same women when they were enjoying a drink-fuelled girls' night out, I guarantee it wouldn't be long before you heard at least one of them guffawing about an ex-boyfriend's tiny penis. Phrases such as 'I'd have had more sitting on a pencil' or 'I had to ask him "Is it in yet?"' would ring through the air, accompanied by much hilarious waving of pinkie fingers. So then, let's dispense with the cosy bullshit and face facts: having a decent-sized penis is very important. Women DO get turned on by it. Men DO have to worry about it. The only real question is, do you?

Well, first off, let's examine where you're putting it. In its dry, unaroused state,[1] the vagina is only about 8cm long, so theoretically a penis of that length should fit quite snugly. When the woman becomes aroused, however, her vagina will expand dramatically in both length and diameter. What doesn't change is the fact that the most sensitive nerve endings in her vagina are near the opening, so it's no surprise to learn that the majority of women hold the girth of a penis to be more important than its length. Get your tape measure out and wrap it around the widest point of your penis, which is usually near the base. The average circumference of an erect cock here is about 11cm, but if you fall short of this benchmark, don't panic — I'll be suggesting several handy remedies later on in this chapter.

As for length, the normal size of an erection falls anywhere between 13cm and 18cm, depending which survey you believe. If you're unlucky enough to measure less than 7cm when hard, then you have what is called — in a remarkably insensitive piece of medical terminology — a 'micropenis'. And the bad news doesn't stop there, I'm afraid. You see all

---

[1] *eg., while its owner is watching movies starring Judd Nelson.*

penises, whatever their size, contain roughly the same amount of nerve endings in the glans at the top. If yours is small, then they'll be concentrated over a smaller area, making you more likely to suffer from over-excitement and premature ejaculation.

Mind you, owning a large cock isn't necessarily a picnic either. Watch a hardcore blue movie and you'll see that guys with really big dicks find it very difficult to get a full-of-blood, pointing-at-the-ceiling hard-on. Anything over 9 inches tends to flop about horizontally, and has to be fed into a woman's private parts indelicately, like putting toothpaste back into a tube. You'll also need to spend a lot more time on foreplay than Joe Average, and certain 'deep penetration' positions will be too uncomfortable for your partner to enjoy — especially as a big tool is more likely to give her a dose of cystitis. Last but not least, research has shown that tight condoms burst more easily than looser fitting ones, so unless you're buying Extra Large down at the chemists, you're more likely to be starting a family by accident or picking up a nasty viral souvenir.

Like the golfer who uses 'the leather wedge' to slyly nudge his ball into a more favourable lie, you'll only be cheating yourself if you don't measure your penis accurately. So avoid the temptation to place the ruler on the scrotum side, as this will falsely add an inch or two. Instead, place it along the top edge and gauge its length from stomach to tip, or — if you don't have a ruler handy — simply hold your erection against this handy chart.

8 inches plus: Well over average. Great to show off in the showers after football (and also a handy bookmark for a literary work of this size), but bear in mind that if your partner is 'small', you're going to have to be very slow and careful in positions like doggy and cowgirl. If you get too abandoned, there's a chance that she might knock an ovary, a painful sensation not dissimilar to you getting kicked in the stones.

7 inches: OK, this is no circus cock, but it's the size that women most commonly describe as 'perfect'. However, don't get too relaxed about it — an equally common female gripe is that men who know they are well hung are lazy when it comes to foreplay.

6 inches: Average. You're unlikely to get any complaints, except from the most ardent of 'size queens'.

4½ inches: Frankly, nothing to write home about. But if you study the sections on 'great foreplay' and 'the best sexual positions for men with a small penis', then your abilities and enthusiasm should keep your partner happy. All the same, it's probably best not to constantly plague her with your insecurities about size — just feel the fear and go for it.

2½ inches or less: Only about 2% of the adult population have penises this small, so you have a pretty stark choice: either live with it and find a woman who is mature enough not to mind, or consider surgical techniques to enlarge it. These are increasingly commonplace procedures among plastic surgeons, so the results are improving in leaps and bounds.

Know your penis

Cowper's gland. This is responsible for the lubrication which appears when you get aroused.[2] It does not contain sperm, but as you can release small amounts of semen before you ejaculate fully, it's best not to get too relaxed about condom use.

The shaft. Quite dull, really.

The frenulum. The small strand of skin which joins the shaft to the glans. Commonly called the Banjo String.

The perineum. The highly sensitive bit of flesh between your scrotum and your anus. Memorably termed 'the biffon' by *Viz* magazine's Roger Melly because, as he so accurately points out, 'it's what your balls biff on'.

The scrotum. Able to rise and fall so as to keep your testicles at optimum temperature, thus enabling them to produce about 1000 new sperm every second.

The urethra. Also called the Jap's Eye, this is the slit through which you pass semen and urine.

[2] *How proud Doctor Cowper's parents must have been when he had this named after him. I bet they ran out and told the whole street.*

The 'clitoris'. It sounds crazy, and in anatomical terms it isn't strictly accurate, but nevertheless men do have an equivalent of the clitoris. (This is because in the early stages a foetus contains both sets of genitals — it only becomes noticeably male or female after about thirteen weeks.) Sited under the surface of the cock, near the bottom end of the frenum, it can give you a very different orgasm if stimulated properly. Ideally, get your partner to press a vibrator on low speed against this area, using a fair bit of pressure. As with her clitoris, it will take time, practice and steady rhythm to achieve results, but they are well worth it for the novelty alone.

The glans. Also known as the helmet, this is the part of the penis which is richest in nerve endings. Like a Hepplewhite chair, it responds well to polishing.[3]

The foreskin. Circumsized cocks are generally held to be 'neater and nicer' by women, but the fact is it will make no appreciable difference to how you perform. The only areas uncut males have to watch out for are hygiene (you need to wash scrupulously under the foreskin) and premature ejaculation (because it is protected from rubbing against your clothes, the nerve endings on an uncircumsized cock can be more sensitive.)

[3] Although not necessarily with Mr Sheen.

When you ejaculate, there are certain things you can do to improve the 'quality' of your semen.

● **Improving the flavour** Clearly important if you expect your girlfriend to swallow. Various foods like garlic and pepper can make your semen taste bitter, so you should avoid these wherever possible if she is complaining. Instead, go for blander foods like potatoes and pasta, or try eating cinnamon toast for breakfast, as this is one of the few foods known to give spunk a sweeter, less tangy flavour. It shouldn't take longer than a week for her to notice the difference. If she has a really hard time swallowing, it might help her if she tries to take the penis deep into her mouth when you come, as the back of the tongue has far fewer tastebuds than the tip.

● **Making it more copious** If the visual element of an orgasm is important to you, then there are several proven ways to ensure that you ejaculate more. Firstly, as semen is mostly composed of water, you should neck plenty of Evian to make sure you're not dehydrated; secondly, get plenty of zinc in your diet (through vitamin supplements or seafood) as this helps sperm production; and lastly, lay off wanking and sex for a few days before each encounter, allowing your 'tanks' to refill. Don't be alarmed if you still fail to live up to the studs in porn movies, however: to refer to two bands allegedly named after ejaculation, the average amount of semen* at orgasm is much nearer to a 'Lovin' Spoonful' than '10cc'.

● **Ejaculating further** Again, this could be important to you if you enjoy spraying your semen over her at orgasm, rather than watching it dribble out pathetically. The best techniques are either to continually stop yourself at the point of climax, thus building up a real head of steam for the final flourish, or to simply bend your cock down when you pull it out before coming. If you then release it upwards like a springboard, your jism will be propelled several feet. Needless to say, this takes a bit of practice and timing to get right.

* Or Pearl Jam, of course.

Exercise your cock

Like any other part of your body, your penis will benefit from regular exercise. Of course, it will continue to function very well even if you sit on the sofa all day wolfing cheeseburgers, but if you really want to get the best from it on those marathon nights of love, you're well advised to keep it in trim.

One of the handiest methods of maintaining a firm and strong erection is to do Kegel exercises, originally developed to help women restore firmness to their vaginas after giving birth. This technique relies on performing a series of 'reps', just like in a Jane Fonda video. (Neatly enough, it's also something that's even more fun if you do it *while* watching a Jane Fonda video.) The muscles you're working are the ones that make your penis go up and down, so get an erection and then flex these so that your cock twitches. Do 25 reps in a session, then move up to 50 as you become more adept, at which point you can also practise maintaining your cock at one angle for a few seconds before letting it relax. The same muscles can be kept in trim by stopping and starting while having a piss, or — if you get off on early Schwarzenegger movies — you can even use the weight of a small towel for resistance. Don't get cocky and overdo it though, because if you attempt to pump anything heavier than a paperback book, you may discover that it's possible to snap your penis. This is a bad thing.

Although it's conceivable that you could do these exercises on the bus or under your desk at work, I'd recommend that you wait until you're alone. If anyone detects you flexing your pelvis in public, rumours will start.

Small penises

We'll be looking at penis enlargement surgery on page 26, but if you'd prefer to try something less radical to make your cock look bigger, then check my ratings on these five popular methods.

Suction devices: Often advertised in the back of pornographic magazines, these operate a bit like a bicycle pump in reverse. You place your erection inside an airtight plastic cylinder and gradually create a vacuum by using the pump. This 'sucking' increases blood flow to the tissue of your cock, which will indeed make it appear larger. The results, however, are temporary, as once

Much ribald humour, but sadly little genuine research, has been devoted to the idea that certain races are better hung than others. For the record, current estimates of the anthropometry of penis size suggest that:

● Men of Asian origin have penises that are, on average, about 2cm shorter than those of their white counterparts.

● Men of African origin can boast an advantage of about 3cm over whites.

● The country which has the largest average cock size is Senegal.

● The Dutch have the longest penises in Europe.

● The Czechs have the fattest penises in Europe.

the device is taken off, your body will quickly seek its normal equilibrium. The dangers of these machines should not be ignored either: I have heard at least one account of a teenager who feel asleep with his pump on, only to find his penis jammed fast and dark purple with uncirculated blood when he woke up in the morning. Not a trip to Casualty that anyone would relish . . .

Pubic grooming: As the top part of your cock is concealed by a 'hanging garden' of pubic hair, you can achieve the illusion of length by clipping this. The best shape to go for is an arrowhead, with the point towards your navel and the remaining hairs hanging down in a 'sideburn' effect, a bit like Noddy Holder's face. To all but the most intense scrutiny, you will now appear to have a penis that's about an inch longer than before. Remember, however, to use only scissors or a razor, as depilatory creams can burn the sensitive skin of the genitals.

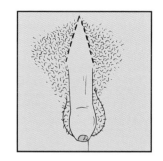

Cock rings: Similar in effect to the vacuum pump, but with the notable advantage that you can keep it on during sex. Cock rings date back to the thirteenth century Orient, where — astonishingly — they were originally made from the eyelashes of slain goats (the hair gave added titillation). Nowadays they come in three basic varieties: the metal and rubber rings, which are not adjustable, and the leather 'snap on' version, which is. Once in place, it will keep the erect penis full of blood, thus maintaining the maximum in length and hardness. The main downside, especially with the metal version, is that you have to wait until your penis is flaccid before removing it. Sometimes this is tricky because of all the trapped blood, and you might have to dunk it in cold water. OK, this is hardly glamorous, but it's a lot better than the alternative, as prolonged constriction can cause thrombosis of the veins.

Lose your gut: The simplest method of all. If you have a bulging waistline, it will (in certain positions, like the missionary) inhibit how much of your penis you can put inside a woman. Just as a fat man can't see much of his cock, so his partner won't be able to feel much.

Wadded condoms: If your partner is really unsatisfied by the girth of your penis, then this is an extreme method that should help you satisfy her. Before putting on a condom, wrap layers of cotton wool around your cock, securing them firmly in place with rubber bands. So long as you stop the wadding a centimetre below the helmet, this should in no way detract from your own pleasure. Unless you feel stupid doing it, of course.

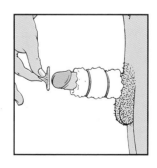

Penis Enlargement

No one these days is surprised by women who have breast implants, and in the next twenty years or so it's likely that penis enlargements will be treated with the same nonchalance. If you're considering it soon however, there are certain facts you need to bear in mind ...

● **How much does it cost?** The average price, depending which method you go for, is about £4,000. No drop in the ocean, admittedly, but as one patient summed it up: 'I used to dream of attracting women by owning a Ferrari. This cost me a fraction of that.'

● **How does it work?** There are two main methods. The first, and simplest, involves making an incision above the base of the penis and cutting the ligament attached to the pubic bone. This adds an inch or so to its length, but adds nothing in girth. The second uses fat cells removed from the stomach, as in a standard liposuction procedure. These are then loaded into a syringe, the needle of which is pushed through a 2cm incision along the entire length of the penis. With a 'tunnel' thus formed inside, the stomach fat is injected and moulded around the cock by the surgeon. This gives extra width.

● **What happens next?** The pain is intense at first, and the penis must remain bandaged for up to a month. There will be permanent scars where the fat was extracted and where the ligament was cut, although these will later be covered to a large extent by pubic hair. It's dangerous for the patient to get aroused at first, so most doctors recommend keeping 'a bag of frozen peas handy to dampen your ardour'.

● **How much bigger will it get?** Current stats suggest that you can add up to 6cm in length and up to 4cm in circumference. Those with the least to start with will gain the most.

● **Any problems?** Frankly, yes. You may need a £1,000 'top up' operation a few months later, as up to 50 per cent of the injected fat may be absorbed back into the body. Also, dying fat cells can cause a nasty inflammation, and there is a high risk of local infection. There is a further chance that the fat may move

around or 'bunch' under your skin, requiring you to massage it back into place after each sexual encounter.

● **Any really nasty problems?** Again, yes. As in most experimental forms of surgery there are quite a few nightmare stories floating around. These vary from the man whose penis actually got smaller because of the way in which the scar tissue healed, to another who was left with an erection that pointed downwards. If you check out your surgeon thoroughly, however, these risks will be greatly reduced.

● **How do I ensure my surgeon is any good?** Sadly, there are no letters which can appear after a surgeon's name to reassure you that he is an expert in penis elongation. The closest you can get is an accreditation awarded by the Royal College of Surgeons for training in plastic or urological surgery generally. When you meet your doctor, interrogate him about his experience in the field, and check up on what he tells you. Ask to see photographs and reports of his work, and be wary of anyone who claims that he can add more than 6cm to your length. Above all, don't be blinded by an address on Harley Street — it contains more sharks than the Miami aquarium.

Penis Problems

Although almost certain to finish well ahead of the dog in any list of Man's Best Friends, the penis can cause problems for its owner. Apart from diseases and serious malfunctions (which will be dealt with in a later chapter — see page 178), the chief ones are performance related. Before the advent of feminism, these could simply be ignored or blamed on the woman, but in the vibrant exciting times we live in it's up to us guys to sort these wrinkles out for ourselves. Here are some handy tips.

● **Coming too soon:** A 'hairtrigger' is the most common sexual complaint that men suffer from. It's usually caused by over-eagerness or anxiety, and though it generally fades with age and experience, it can develop into a serious mental block.

To find out how you rate, you first need to know what a 'normal' length of time to last is. Well, the obvious answer would be 'long enough to make sure you and your partner are both satisfied', and if you assume that the average timespan for a woman to come during sex is about twenty minutes, then that's what you should be aiming for. (Interestingly enough, however, a bed-manufacturing company once did some research on the springing of their mattresses which involved strapping a 'thrustometer' — basically, a jogger's pedometer held in place by a garter — to the thighs of love-making couples. The average number of thrusts in a sex session was only 93.)

If you come up short in this department, then you might consider any of these techniques:

Stopping and starting. When you feel that you are nearing the point of no return, pull out of her vagina and pause for a few seconds until the urgency has receded. You can even turn this to mutual advantage by using the time to give her stimulation with your mouth or hand, or manoeuvring each other into a new position.

Change your thrust. Rather than just going in and out, try leaving your cock deep within her and moving your hips in a figure-of-eight pattern instead. This will provide pleasant friction for her as you grind your body against her pubic area, but leave your sensitive glans relatively unstimulated.

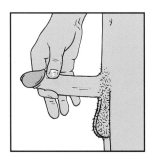

The tart squeeze. Named after a technique popular among prostitutes (although why they would wish their clients to last longer is anyone's guess), this can be done by either you or your partner. When you feel close to orgasm, take your cock out and using the thumb and fingers of one hand, squeeze it quite hard just below the rim. This technique will work better — and maybe be less painful — if you practise getting the pressure right while masturbating on your own.

The perineum press. A similar, if slightly more gymnastic version of the above. Get her to press hard on your perineum, pushing it upwards as though into your body.

Masturbating beforehand. Brilliant in its simplicity, this will ensure that you take longer to come when you have sex. However, timing is everything, because if you leave it too near to the wire before wanking, you may not be able to perform at all.

Alcohol and sedatives. These will both slow you down, but it may be a case of cutting off your nose to spite your face, because they can also make you suffer from brewer's droop.[4]

Stick to the missionary. As you are more in control of the thrusting in this position, you will be better able to dictate the pace and slow things down when necessary.

Think about bad things. An old chestnut, yes, but nevertheless some people have achieved good results by doing complex mathematical problems in their heads while shagging. If you're no good at algebra, another popular version is to imagine that your girlfriend is shouting, 'Yes, O Mighty Life Giver, make me big with child.' The thought of a four-year stretch changing nappies certainly works wonders for me, anyway.

● **Not coming for ages:** Although this would seem to be an advantage, especially as it gives the woman more time to climax, it can be a real problem for some men as they get older. Stress and tiredness are common causes, and the condition can also be exacerbated if you're taking anti-depressants or certain anti-histamine drugs prescribed for colds and sinus problems. Alcohol and cocaine can also slow down the time it takes to come, so lay off these before sex if it's a worry. Some men will claim they lose vital sensitivity when using a condom, often berating their partner with expressions like, 'I'm sorry, I just can't feel anything when I have one on.' This can easily be disproved by the woman in question if she replies, 'OK, if you can't feel anything, then you won't mind if I hit your cock with the sharp edge of a ruler.'

● **Not getting it up:** A failure to get wood happens to us all at one time or another. Clearly, one reason for it is that you simply don't fancy your partner at that particular time, but it can also be because you fancy her too much. This sounds insane, but I speak from personal experience. I once adored a woman so much that I began to think, 'I can't put my cock in *her*. I mean, I know where it's *been*.' Luckily, good old male lust is pretty much certain to override this sort of sensitivity before long, and once you've broken your duck, it should disappear entirely.

　　If your inability to get a hard on is more of a physical problem, then you

---

[4] *Or, indeed, pharmacist's flop.*

should be able to get Viagra prescribed, the results of which — as literally dozens of *Daily Mail* feature writers have attested — are remarkably effective. If it does fail, however, you might consider taking prostoglandin, a drug which is injected into the base of the penis and which is often used by porn stars when they're having difficulty getting that last scene in the can. This isn't available on prescription in Britain, so getting hold of it may involve talking to a shady man in an alleyway or making friends with a doctor, but it isn't particularly dangerous. My father, who although not, sadly, a porn star, is one of the world's leading toxicologists, assures me that 'it's a naturally occurring cytokyne which is already present in the body, and acts as a chemical messenger to the brain.'[5] Also it was most famously used by celebrity breadknife victim John Wayne Bobbitt in his hardcore debut *Uncut*, and you'd think that he, of all people, would be careful what he did to his penis.

● **Not getting it down:** A permanent erection (known as priapism, after one of the better hung Greek gods) might sound like a great idea, but it's actually very painful and embarrassing. The most common victims are long distance lorry drivers, whose genitals are constantly stimulated into semi-stiffness by the vibrations of their vehicle, giving rise to a condition known as 'diesel penis'. This makes it tricky for them to achieve full erections while having sex, and is best treated by seeing a sex therapist. Or getting a desk job, of course.

Other Erogenous Zones

As if having a penis to play with at night wasn't proof enough of God's bounty,[6] He has also seen fit to equip us with several other 'pleasure centres'. You will doubtless discover these in the normal course of love-making, but just in case you've been playing things very straight, here are some highlights to watch out for:

---

[5] *We also talk a lot about football.*
[6] *Leviticus 4:18.*

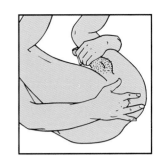

● **The G-spot:** Situated just a couple of inches inside your rectum is your prostate gland which, when properly handled, can intensify your climax. It's no walk in the park to play with on your own, but if you want to find out what it feels like before letting your lover loose on it, then try lying on your back with your knees pulled up to your chest. In this position, you should be able to easily insert a finger and press it against the front wall of your arse. When you discover something that feels a bit like a walnut, massage it gently in a downwards direction. If you're agile and ambidextrous enough, try to masturbate while doing this. As well as doubling your pleasure, you may even find that when you ejaculate the semen comes in a continuous stream rather than in spurts.

Getting your partner to do it while she's fellating you off is a lot simpler, of course. But make sure she'd clipped her nails first, or you could risk catching an infection.

● **The nipples:** Some men can't feel anything in 'em; some can. If you're one of the latter, not only will you be able to get extra fun out of sex, but you'll also gain a valuable insight into how a woman likes her nipples to be aroused. Don't be afraid to experiment with different pressures and textures, as objects as various as feathers and sandpaper will provide intense stimulation.

● **The perineum:** Not to be ignored by the accomplished fellatrix, when this is lightly caressed it can send thrilling ripples through the whole of the 'downtown business district'. If she can also gently squeeze and 'juggle' the balls while doing this, so much the better.

● **The toes:** It isn't only Fergie who likes having her toes sucked,[7] as you'll discover if you let your babe give you a foot job. The action is the same as if she was sucking you off, and it's best if she reaches forward and masturbates you at the same time. Clearly, if her enjoyment of this act is at all important to you, you should cut your toenails first. And get all the dirt out of them with a penknife too.

---

[7] *Although with her it would admittedly be that much harder to tell just which piggy went to market.*

31

KNOW HER BODY

No matter how baffling our behaviour may be to the ladies, at least we men can proudly boast that our genitals are right out there in the open and easy to see. This is not so with women: their sex organs seem to have been hidden with the ingenuity of Anne Frank, contain parts that have to be handled with the dexterity usually reserved for the manufacture of Swiss watches, and — final proof, surely, that God has a crappy sense of humour — are disguised by a thick bush of pubic hair. It is, quite literally, a jungle in there. But if you want to be good in bed, you've got to hack your way through that jungle, making mental maps of each twist and contour, mastering the most efficient route to your goal, navigating the rapids of uncertainty and clumsiness until you can say, at last and with confidence, 'Ah, Dr Clitoris, I presume.'[8]

Absolute bollocks aside, it is clearly important that you learn all about your lover's pussy. No two women are the same, and the appearance of their genitals and the way they like them to be aroused are just as varied. Thus, unless you've been faithful to one partner for ages, and you know instinctively by now how to take her to heaven and back,[9] you're going to need to find out how each new woman works.

The best way to do this, of course, is to ask. But, unless your date's idea of a fun night in involves giving a gynaecological lecture, possibly with slides, you'll have to do this in a subtle way. In my experience, lines like 'I really want to please you, so don't be shy about telling me what you want' and 'Show me how you like it' will do the trick, although you should stop short of asking for detailed, *Golden Shot* style directions unless you want to kill the mood.

It's also good advice not to get too cheesy about the whole process, especially if it's the first time you've gone to bed together. I know those brick-thick romantic novels women get off on are full of stuff like 'Sir Rodney leant closer to her and murmured, "It's beautiful. You're opening up like a flower,"' but in the real world chicks will probably puke if you say this. They're not dumb. They've looked in the mirror, and they're well aware that what they sit on looks more like one of those grim South American plants which eat insects than the sort of thing that wins prizes at a horticultural fair.

Similarly, if you're going to be asking her intimate questions, you've got to use the right terminology. This is tricky, and it'll vary from woman to woman, but to give you a rough notion of what's acceptable, I've conducted a straw poll of forty-three girls I know. Opposite are their views on ten commonly-used names:

---

[8] *And I get paid to write this stuff.*
[9] *Usually via a shoe shop.*

THE RIGHT TERMINOLOGY

vagina ('Too medical... I'd feel like I was being examined by a doctor');

beaver ('That's a guy word... I don't know any woman who calls it that... it doesn't look anything like a beaver');

pussy ('That's fine... it's sweet but not sickly... I use it');

it ('OK in passing, but not for regular use... a bit impersonal... sounds like he's afraid of sex');

there ('Fine... I call it that... good if he says "I want to touch you there," but not very passionate, is it?');

growler ('That's a Denise Van Outen word... it's cute... doesn't sound very pretty");

snatch ('Horrible, horrible, horrible... I'd consider kicking a man out of bed for saying that');

cunt ('Fine, so long as it's dirty sex... you know that's what they want to call it anyway');

muff ('That's nicely neutral... inoffensive... nothing wrong with it');

fanny ('A bit old fashioned... not bad... terrible if she's called Frances, otherwise it'll do').

So then, sports fans, it looks like 'pussy', 'muff' and 'cunt' are on the podium, with 'growler' and 'there' bubblin' under. But so long as you are sensitive enough to change your vocabulary immediately to what pleases her, and steer clear of 'snatch', you won't get your marching orders.

Know her pussy

The labia: The two sets of lips which form the outside of her vagina, these are called the labia majora and the labia minora. But only by doctors or people who really want to show off about that Latin 'O' level they passed: to you and me they're the outer and inner lips. Usually, the outer ones will cover the inner, but it's not uncommon for those to hang down outside. As she gets aroused, the inner lips will swell and thicken with blood, often going red, and they'll secrete a lubricant to ease the entry of your cock. Or whatever else she's intending to put in there.

The mons pubis: More Latin, I'm afraid, this time translating as 'pubic mountain'.[10] In essence, it's the cushion of flesh under her bush, which serves as a handy buffer when you're shagging.

Urethra: Situated just above the vaginal opening, this is the tiny hole where girls pee from. As well as providing no sexual thrills, it's absolutely useless for writing your name in the snow.

Perineum: As for guys, this area is rich in nerve-endings, and the sophisticated lover will pay it due attention when pleasuring his befancied.

Clitoris: The main pleasure centre of a woman — but remember that it's not the only one, so take time to detour over the rest of her body rather than heading straight for here. The external part of the clitoris which, like certain types of sports cars, is covered in a retractable hood, can vary in size from a grain of rice to a baked bean, but it's actually part of a larger organ which extends inside the body. It's not always easy to find, or even to see, so learn to decode your lover's moans and she'll let you know when you've hit paydirt.

The G-spot: Discovered by a kraut, but don't let that put you off,[11] this is a small, spongy region hidden (wouldn't it have to be) a couple of inches inside the vagina. It's on the front wall, which is to say the side nearest her stomach, and some sex researchers claim that it can produce orgasms even without clitoral stimulation. Mind you, just as many other experts claim it doesn't exist at all, so you're pretty much on your own with this one.

The vagina: A muscle-lined cylinder that will expand the more turned on she gets. The inside feels slightly 'ribbed', and this makes penetration more exciting, especially if she has enough control to 'milk' your penis. Although that old saw about 'no penis being too big for a woman's vagina because it expands enough to have a baby' is true so far as girth goes, be aware that it is quite possible for a long cock to jab painfully against the neck of her womb. So go easy if your nickname is 'Arkle'.

---

[10] *And how much more fun Sunday morning television would be if* The Waltons *had been set there.*

[11] *Although when you learn that the German word for nipple is* Brustwarze *(literally 'breastwart'), you may feel disinclined to take any sexual tips from our sausage-swilling chums.*

OK, so now you know how to ask her where her clitoris is. But your problems aren't over. Oh no, not by a long chalk. You see, unlike your cock, which responds pretty readily to any simple up and down motion, her 'ideal pressure point' and the way she likes it to be stimulated may vary from hour to hour. Her libido is also much more in thrall to her emotional and mental state than yours (which, let's face it, is usually happy to summon up a hard-on at short notice, even at funerals).

This being the case, she will need to offer more than an occasional murmur of approval if she wants to use you as a stud-like provider of orgasms. The most important step she can take here is to masturbate regularly. Thanks to the efforts of magazines like *Cosmopolitan*,[12] of course, most modern girls do this, but there are still plenty around who find it seedy or disgusting. If your lover falls into this camp, then it's best to encourage her discreetly. Don't, for pity's sake, give her a copy of one of those porn mags for women which feature heavily oiled beefcakes wearing nothing but a limp dick and a year's supply of Cossack hairspray. Instead, 'accidentally' leave a copy of one of Nancy Friday's red–hot collections of women's fantasies in her bathroom, and let her imagination do the rest. Once she begins to masturbate, it will teach her what she likes and dislikes, and this knowledge will make it easier for her to have orgasms when she's with you.

Porn movies, too, can be a good educational tool for curious couples. If you steer clear of the lousy ones featuring large, selfish, moustachioed Germans — and most XXX video shop owners will be happy to give you a preview of what's on a tape before you buy it — you'll find that these flicks will show you, at the very least, some good ideas. (And even if your lover says 'Oh, what he's doing there is gross!' you'll have learnt something about what *not* to do.) Sure, some old-fashioned or radically feminist women may veto this approach, but they'll only be doing themselves harm in the long run. If this is a problem, then there are many 'right on' porn movies directed by women which, although featuring less dialogue like 'Reite mich! Reite mich, du Starker Gaul!'[13] than is customary, are much more feminist-friendly.

---

[12] *Typical cover line: 'Have a multiple orgasm and lose two stone!'*
[13] *'Ride me! Ride me, you big horse!'*

35

If you try all these methods and you're still missing the target, then your girlfriend might consider two slightly more direct shortcuts to clitoral identification. The first involves shaving her pubic hair off so you can see things more clearly. This might be a bit itchy for her when the stubble starts to grow back, but if it's going to make her sex life better then this is a pretty small price to pay. (She probably gets her bikini line waxed before going on holiday anyway, and that is far more painful.) It's not an easy job, mind you, so she may ask for some help. If so, then start by trimming most of the hairs off with a pair of small scissors, using a comb to keep the blades away from the skin. Then splash on some warm water and shaving foam, and use a razor *very carefully*, especially near the clitoris. Apply some balm or aloe vera afterwards to stop her getting a shaving rash. If this is too scary for her, she can use a depilatory cream. She's a woman — she'll know which ones are best. Lastly, when she's been trimmed, make sure you tell her that you find it attractive, even if you don't, because she's made a sacrifice for you here.

The second method sounds absurd, but it's even more effective. Next time she masturbates, ask her to dip her fingers in vegetable dye. Like the saffron that Sikh women use on their foreheads, this is harmless but will mark the 'target' for a few days before washing off naturally. Mind you, if she loves you enough to walk round with a bright green, peppermint-flavoured clitoris, you're going to have to keep your end of the bargain up and really give her a lot of top-notch foreplay while it lasts.

Other Erogenous Zones

Of course, with the possible exception of Mrs Slocombe in Are You Being Served?, *there is more to pleasuring a woman than stroking her pussy. In fact her whole body is a minefield of erogenous zones, and you've got to know how to set off the right explosions.[14] Here, just in case you haven't noticed, are the main areas of interest:*

● **The neck:** Not just a handy target for when Henry VIII wanted to avoid all that bothersome paperwork with the Child Support Agency, it's also the number

---

[14] © Barry White.

one place to get a woman's motor revving. Kisses here, if ticklish and feathery enough, will send shivers straight down her spine. But keep it light: she doesn't want to feel your slobber dribbling down her collar.

● **The ears:** Another delicacy, but one you have to treat with respect, as it will definitely not turn her on if you start snarfing on her lugholes like they were Quavers. Instead, try ultra-light nibbling on the lobe (so long as she's not wearing earrings) and the outer edge, alternating this with soft, hot breaths over the whole area. If you've got a nice pointy tongue like that bloke out of Kiss, you can even dart it gently in and out of the hole. Clearly, you'll have to hold her hair out the way with one hand, and it'll be best for you if her ear doesn't contain enough wax to house a colony of bees.

● **The breasts:** Needless to say, touching her breasts will be very exciting for you as well as for her, so there's no excuse for not paying them maximum attention. The golden rule is to start softly as the last thing she wants is some guy attacking her lallies as though they were a dangerous judo opponent. So, begin by caressing the 'valley' between them, then gently cup them in your hands. As you progress, build up the pressure of your squeeze until she lets you know what's perfect. A dab of oil will help things run along even more smoothly and sexily, and you should take care to give both of them equal attention. Crazy as it seems, many women attribute 'personalities' to their boobs, and they may each need different treatment.

● **The nipples:** Once you have fondled her breasts, move on to the nipples. Try circling your fingers around the breasts until they zero in on the areola (the browny-pink bit around the nipple), then gently strumming them. You can also squeeze them or softly flick them between finger and thumb, but avoid any prodding or 'radio tuning' moves, as she'll feel like a piece of unreliable hi-fi equipment. Using your mouth, try blowing on them, then sucking them into your mouth, letting your lips and tongue wet them. Keep your teeth out of things — unless she tells you she prefers 'rough' stimulation — and imagine that you're giving her breast a mini blow job. Above all, just because you're sucking one nipple, don't forget to use your hand on the other one.

● **The back:** Massage is a bore, and in my opinion best left to the Swedes and Turks, but if you can manage to put in five minutes or so of back rubbing, it'll really help to relax your lover. Use a bit of scented oil or baby lotion, slam on some soothing music, and alternate soft stroking with finger kneading. You

37

Talking about sex

If you and your girlfriend both want to get the most enjoyment possible out of sex, then it's vital that you're able to communicate your desires. But, even though you both see each other naked a lot, this can be embarrassing. Face it, you probably feel iffy about criticising her technique, because you know how badly you'd be pissed off if she complained about all your hard work under the counterpane. However, this isn't the Middle East peace negotiations we're talking about, so if you follow these simple guidelines you should be able to have a meaningful dialogue . . .

● **When to talk.** There's a time and a place to discuss these matters, and clearly you should make sure that it happens when you're both alone and comfortable. (Mooting her sexual failings to a rapt dinner party audience may be amusing, but it's going to result in a trip to Siberia for your genitals.) Personally, I don't think you can beat bed as a venue, but you should talk about it before anything sexual starts happening rather than just afterwards. Because it'll sound too pissy and critical then.

● **Keep it inoffensive.** The key note to strike is one of encouragement rather than criticism. Explain to her that what she does is just great, but that it would be even better if she tried such-and-such. NEVER begin a sentence with the words, 'Well, my ex-girlfriend had this amazing trick...', as she'll feel inadequate in comparison. Similarly, gently explain to her that you're asking how to turn her on better because you're so crazy about her, not because you're implying that she's unresponsive.

● **How to demonstrate.** If your conversation here is to have any lasting effect, you'll need to be frank. And as it's sometimes difficult to explain these things in words, you're best bet is to demonstrate. If you're both naked and warmed up, spend half an hour experimenting with techniques, as this will be a huge turn-on as well as educational. If the mood is wrong for something that full on, however, you can use a lighter method. If, say, you want to show her how you like to be fellated, practise on her thumb until she knows the right speed and pressure for you. Similarly, if she needs to tell you how hard to touch her clitoris, she can rub her fingers on any sensitive part of your body, with the palm of the hand being a favourite.

● **Putting it into practice.** Of course, like any exam, one lesson probably won't be enough to learn everything you need. So continue the learning process when you're making love. Again, keep a sense of fun about it, giggling if she gets it wrong rather than going 'No! No! No! How many times do I have to show you, woman?' Once you've established the necessary level of trust and comfort, you'll be able to try new things out on the hoof, rather than having to sit down for another conference first. And then you're both smiling.

don't need to know anything about pressure points or physiotherapy — just be gentle and try not to say, 'I've been doing this for ages, are you horny yet?'

● **The thighs:** Stroking and kissing the thighs and the back of the knees before touching her pussy will pay dividends. Your best bet is to skirt around her pubic area, getting closer and closer, but then teasingly pulling away until she's howling for it.

Her Orgasm

It might seem premature to be discussing her orgasm at this stage, especially as — in sexual terms — we've barely covered the mechanics of getting her coat off, but I figure there's no harm in being aware of what you're aiming for. And a woman's orgasm is a far more complex thing than the eager, easy jolt you and I enjoy so much.

For a start, while men can have orgasms pretty much at will, hers will require more than merely supplying the correct physical stimulation. She'll almost certainly have to be in a receptive frame of mind as well. (And, though I know I promised not to bombard you with statistics, the laboratory research figures show that fewer than 1 in 10 women can be made to 'trigger' an orgasm involuntarily.) Mind you, I don't know your girlfriend,[15] and I have no idea whether she gets turned on by you reading her sonnet sequences or rubbing grapefruit in her face, so getting her into the appropriate mental state is completely down to you. The physical side of things, however, goes like this:

Women can have two kinds of orgasm. The first, and most common, is the clitoral orgasm, brought on — as the name cunningly suggests — by direct stimulation of her clitoris. This will happen mostly through foreplay; only in very few sexual positions is the clitoris angled correctly to get rubbed against the shaft of your thrusting cock.

Her climax will follow certain set stages: arousal, when she gets wet and

---

[15] *Though if she's reading this, and she's cute, I'd just like to say: 'Hi. Sagittarius?'*

her labia fill with blood; plateau, where her sensations of pleasure flatten out before the climb to orgasm; orgasm itself, which lasts about ten seconds, and in which her vagina will be subject to spasms and muscular contractions; and post-climax, where she'll slowly float down from the ceiling again. Once she's come, she probably won't want to be touched, as her clitoris will be incredibly sensitive.

The second kind of orgasm is the vaginal one, which only about 20 per cent of women claim to have. Caused by the sensations she feels inside her pussy, and probably directly linked to G-spot stimulation, it's less dramatic and characterised more by a warm glow of contentment throughout the body than any banshee shrieking and bucking about.

When they come, some women may also ejaculate liquid. While this is alarming if you happen to be going down on her at the time, it's nothing to make a fuss about. In some cases, the liquid will be involuntarily ejected urine, in which instance you should advise her to take a pee before coming to bed next time; in others it will be a clear, viscous fluid that hails from some glands near the G-spot.

Is she faking?

If you've been going out with a woman for a long time and she always appears to come when you have sex, then I'm sorry, chum, but there's a strong chance some of her orgasms are an act. This doesn't mean your technique is lousy: it could just be that sometimes she realises early doors that she's not going to reach a climax, and so she pretends in order to stop you going on for hours. If it really bugs you not knowing the truth, however, these are the physiological signs of a woman's progress towards real orgasm.

● When you start turning her on, her pulse rate will quicken and her nipples become erect.

● Next, you should feel her clitoris become erect, her pussy become lubricated, and her labia minora enlarge.

● On the brink of coming, her clitoris will shorten, the colour of her labia will deepen, and the areola will swell.

● As she hits the treble 20, her breathing will become shallower and her vaginal muscles will spasm. Don't be fooled by cries of 'Ohgodohgodohgod!' though, as they don't necessarily mean anything. She could do those on the *bus*.

● Right after orgasm, some women will get a momentary pinkish rash across their chest.

● If you think she's faking, try touching her clitoris right afterwards. If she can bear hard pressure on its tip, the smart money says she's doing a Meg Ryan.

MASTURBATION

Although this book is concerned with giving the women in your life more pleasure, you shouldn't forget to look after the wonderful human being that is you as well. And it's a stone cold fact that, throughout the course of your life, you'll make love to yourself far more often than you will to girls. Disagree? Well, take a minute to think about it — about all those midnight sessions as a teenager, with a veteran copy of *Mayfair* pulled from its hiding place and the blankets tented above your knees; all those nights as an adult when you couldn't get a date; the times when you were horny, or lonely, or just plain bored. And even when you had a steady partner, let's be honest, there were still many occasions when a wank was a far more tempting option than going through the whole rigmarole of sex. Just wait until she's asleep, then bingo — no pressure, no effort, no having to tell her how great she was afterwards. And these numbers add up. They add up to the conclusion that — statistically speaking, at least — the love of your life is your right hand.

This being a fact, you then have to wonder why wanking is such an unimaginative process. Time after time, we use the same old up and down technique. We even lie in the same position. If a woman was this boring in bed, we'd dump her within weeks, but the uncritical love affair with our wrist will endure for half a century or more.

But it doesn't have to be that way. There are plenty of novel methods — not all of them involving battery-powered accessories — which can spice things up when you're flying solo.[16] Starting with the simpler techniques, we come first to the **Numb Arm**, which I first heard about from a submariner friend of mine. He was just back from a four month tour of duty — basically, an undersea jaunt to test out whether our nuclear missiles are a worthwhile deterrent[17] — and he told me that his colleagues voted this the most effective way to stave off boredom. What you do is shave the hair off your right hand, paint the nails with a becoming varnish such as 'Evening in Venice', and then lie with your whole bodyweight on your arm until it's numb. Next you pick up the flopping, insensate limb, mould the fingers into a grip around your old fella, and then

---

[16] *This is what we professional writers call a 'metaphor'. I am in no way suggesting that the pilots of light aircraft masturbate while at the controls.*

[17] *And the good news is, taxpayers, that they experienced absolutely no trouble at all from fish.*

move it up and down with your left hand. Having tried it, I can confirm that it does indeed feel as though you are being wanked off by a complete stranger. Although, admittedly, one who is not particularly good at giving hand jobs.

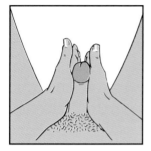

Slightly less labour-intensive is the **Pastry Roll**, in which you replace the normal hand grip with a style that uses the palms of both hands. What you do is put your hands on the sides of your shaft, and — with the fingers held out straight — rub them back and forwards as though rolling, yes, some pastry into a long tubular shape. (Because you need a bit of room to work, this is best attempted when you're either standing up or lying flat on your back.) The sensation is highly exciting and it builds up until your cock feels very warm. At this point you can either bring yourself off in the usual way, or use your top two 'rolling fingers' to softly tug up and down around your helmet.

Moving on, we come to the **Yugoslavian Wank**, a perversion named — for unfathomable reasons[18] — after the country whose citizens seem to have sadly misunderstood the meaning of the phrase 'we all get on like a house on fire'. To do this properly, you need to be quite supple, so if you can't get anywhere near the lotus position save yourself some trouble and skip this paragraph. Right then, when you masturbate, do it sitting up, with your feet tucked up near your scrotum, and place your erection between your in-turned soles. Rock back and forth, and you will experience not only enough friction on your penis to make you come, but also all the soothing benefits of a foot spa. Guys who lack the flexibility to manage this — and who haven't, as clearly instructed, gone on to the next section — can try a compromise. Instead of sitting up, lie on your back (it's easier on the hamstrings) and put your cock between your ankles instead of your soles. Sure, they're a bit too bony, but you can neutralise this by wearing some of those thick woolly socks favoured by the rambling community.

And talking of socks, I might as well mention that old chestnut of a masturbation technique, long-beloved of people who don't want to make a stain on their sheets, the **Sock Wank**. It is brilliant in its simplicity: all you have to do is hold a sock over your old fella while having a tug. Exhaustive tests at Casa Smith suggest that silk, cotton and wool socks provide the nicest feel, although those tantalised by the possibilities of static shock can charge nylon hosiery by rubbing it over other man-made fibres beforehand. On a basic hygiene theme,

---

[18] *Although it could be because their most famous citizen, Marshal Tito, is the only world leader ever whose name contains a rude bodypart[19]. Unless you count President Canaan Banana of Zimbabwe, of course.*
[19] *And don't forget, it used to be spelt JUGoslavia.*

in case anyone from France is reading this, it's essential to a) use a clean sock, and b) remember not to put it on when you're rushing to work the next morning. If you forget to throw it in the wash basket and your girlfriend finds it on the floor later that week, it is vital — for both your fragile egos — that you tell her a lie. If she learns that you enjoy making love to laundry in your spare time, she'll be out of there faster than Linford Christie with a firework up his arse, so just say you had a cold last night, and you couldn't find anything else to blow your nose on. That, too, is disgusting, but it's not a sacking offence.

No amount of fast talking, however, will earn you a reprieve if she catches you in the act of trying out the **Bicycle Wank**. Many teenagers — well, certainly the more optimistic ones — will probably have attempted this already, as it's actually a refinement on autofellatio. As in that doomed endeavour, you lie on your back and swing your legs above you, just like 'cycling in the air' during gym class. Your cock dips tantalisingly close to your lips but, unless your tongue is as long as an anteater's, all you're going to get is a close up. Don't give up using your hand, however, because you can still indulge in a vaguely pervy role play, where you get to feel like a woman feels when you come in her face. This is obviously a big male power trip (which maybe explains why so few women are prepared to do it), and the psychological effects are as interesting as the lumbar ones are painful. It certainly gave me a new angle on orgasm, and it also boosted my ego because — for a change — my cock looked enormous and frightening. That said, the dénouement is tricky: as in Jim Bowen's *Bullseye*, the skill lies in keeping your ejaculation 'out of the black' (i.e. your hair and eyes) and 'into the red' (your skin) to avoid the necessity for a long hot shower. And temporary blindness.

Now we move on to masturbation gimmicks that require the use of props. Luckily all these are readily available in the comfort and luxury of your own home so their presence will not cause alarm to visitors, but you'd still be well advised to make sure the front door is locked before giving them a whirl.

Kicking us off is the **Wet Sofa.** Popular among American 'frat house' students, this involves getting hold of a child's water wing, rubbing the inside edge with a copious lathering of Vaseline, and then jamming it between the base and the cushions of your sofa. Thus equipped, you kneel down in the doggy-style position and hump away. It's actually surprisingly easy to vary the grip and the speed of thrusting, and you will face only three small problems. Firstly, unless you're a dwarf, you may need to prop up the legs of your settee with blocks of wood to get the angle right. Secondly, you must maintain sufficient downward pressure on the cushion, otherwise the water wing gradually slides back to that gap where all the loose change and bits of fluff have accumulated. Lastly, there's

the actual moment of ejaculation. Now that Ikea have insisted that everyone 'chucks out their chintz', sofas tend to come in primary colours, none of which take a semen stain quite like a nice, complicated pattern of garden flowers used to do. You thus have to whip it out at the climactic moment and fuss about with tissues, which kills things a little.

Altogether simpler is the budget version of this, also a popular diversion on Her Majesty's submarines, and known as the **Wet Loo Roll**. You take the cardboard tube from a roll of Andrex, slather the inside with plenty of lubricant, and shuttle it up and down your member. True aficionados will not settle for mere Vaseline or K-Y Jelly, however, and apparently great results have been achieved by using that rough, granular face lotion that is usually employed to flake away dead skin cells.

Moving into the home straight, we come to masturbatory variations which involve the use of food. Sex fans of a literary bent may already be aware of the scene in *Portnoy's Complaint* where the young Jewish hero entertains himself with a piece of raw liver, but there is actually a more effective literary precedent — the **Charles Bukowski Cocktail**. Invented by the celebrated author of that name, this is one recipe which will never appear on *Can't Cook, Won't Cook*, much to the dismay of those of us who would like to see Ainsley Harriott shut up for once. To prepare it you need:

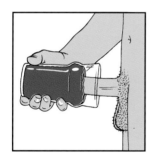

> *A quarter pound of mince*
> *A carton of eggs*
> *A beer glass*

When you have collected these, whisk the raw eggs and mince together until they are moist to the touch, then fill the beer glass with them. Insert your penis and thrust in and out until you come. Of course, some people may find that putting their private parts anywhere near breakable glass is a turn-off, in which case they would be well advised to use Tupperware instead.

Lastly, there is the novel sensation that can only be provided by the **Ben & Jerry Wank**. It's a real gem. Fill the tip of a condom with cold ice cream, then slip it on and start strumming. The whole of your bell end will freeze up, making it go weirdly numb, but as a result your sperm, when you eventually climax, will come out feeling hotter than molten lead. If all goes to plan, you can even refreeze it and serve it up to your tyrannical boss next time he pops over for dinner.

What do butt plugs do?

For the masturbator who is really eager to take things to the edge, and who is still unsatisfied after raping his sofa and trying all the other methods I've suggested, butt plugs could be worth a pop. Designed especially to fit the anus, and fitted with a flanged end so they don't disappear up inside you, they will add stimulus to your prostate gland (or male G-spot). Variations on this theme include 'Siamese Strings', which consist of a thread to which rubber balls have been attached, a bit like fishing weights. These are inserted up the tradesman's entrance, and then pulled out as you climax. Also worthy of note are 'Ass Eggs', an American invention which comprises two or more metal balls, worn for day-long sensual excitement when the owner is, say, riding a motorbike.

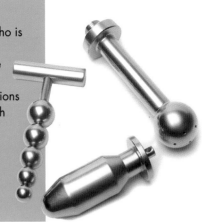

Masturbation techniques to avoid

Although I am absolutely the last person to criticise men for taking sexual pleasure in any way they choose,[20] it's important to realise that there are certain tempting masturbation techniques you would do well to avoid.

● **Vacuum cleaners:** Yes, they're cylindrical. Yes, they are the most efficient sucking devices known to man. But no, they will not give you an amazing blow-job. The *British Medical Journal* of July 1980 contains several case studies of men who have ended up on the operating table as a result of making this mistake, unaware that most vacuum cleaners have fan blades positioned only 15cm from the outlet. Although the ensuing lacerations can be stitched up without too much permanent damage, the really painful bit is coming up with an excuse for how your cock got there in the first place. My own personal

---

[20] *Beating Hugh Hefner in a closely fought final.*

favourite is the sixty-year-old man who claimed he was 'changing the plug on the cleaner while my wife was out shopping, when it suddenly turned itself on just as my dressing gown fell open and sucked my penis inside'.

● **Scarfing:** Also known as 'autoerotic asphyxiation', this was widely rumoured to have lead to the death of INXS singer Michael Hutchence. Practitioners tighten a scarf or rope around their neck while they are masturbating, getting off on the light-headedness this causes and the surge of adrenalin produced by the body as it senses a life-threatening condition. Needless to say, this can go horribly wrong if you black out, and hospital estimates suggest that it accounts for the deaths of over 500 men a year worldwide.

● **Pipe cleaners:** Admirable though they may be for sweeping the St Bruno out of your grandad's churchwarden, pipe cleaners are not suitable for inserting down your urethra while wanking. The theory behind this pursuit is that it stimulates the tender nerve-endings inside your penis, but it can also lead to cuts, bladder damage, and even invasive surgery if the pipe cleaner gets trapped. Again, the only people who are going to get any real pleasure from this in the long run are the staff of your local Casualty department, who may well video the operation to show at their Christmas party.

CHAPTER 3 *foreplay*

The Victorian era was in many ways a great one to live through. We had an empire that stretched around the globe, much of it acquired simply in exchange for brightly coloured beads; we'd invented trains, but not yet come up with excuses for them arriving late; Germany didn't exist; and a man could grow a large, bushy moustache without strangers nudging each other and whispering 'Clapham Common'. However one thing ruins the magnificence of this picture — the fact that nineteenth century women had to 'shut their eyes and think of England' at bedtime.[1] It would appear that, as with Australian men today, our ancestors' foreplay technique consisted of taking off their slippers and saying, 'Brace yourself, love.'

Thankfully, of course, we've made great strides since then. Through sex education, we are aware that it takes the average man about three minutes to come, but that the average woman needs twenty minutes. Even more encouragingly, most of us are now clued up to the fact that the solution to this disparity is not to send your girlfriend upstairs with an erotic novel and a long-handled hairbrush, then ask her to give you a shout after seventeen minutes. No, we recognise that there's a job to be done, and that we have to do it.

---

[1] This was especially annoying for the Welsh.

There is still, mind you, a world of difference between trying to give good foreplay and actually succeeding. So let's kick off this vast section by laying down some ground rules. For a start, there's the word itself: foreplay. This suggests that kissing, stroking, biting and licking are activities that should be attempted only *before* sex, whereas the lover seeking plaudits should be prepared to do them throughout the whole performance, from soup to nuts. And afterwards, too. Bear in mind also that getting into a set routine is lethal to passion, so instead of going through your regular moves each time as though they had been choreographed as rigidly as a minuet, mix things up. Begin foreplay way before you intend to go to bed, teasing her for hours with kisses and caresses, stopping and starting until she is really fired up and raring to set the sheets ablaze. When you're in bed, punctuate each break between positions with cunnilingus or fingerwork, and — especially if you have a small cock — try to make sure she comes at least once before you do.

Above all, when you are caressing her breasts and private parts, keep this motto in the forefront of your mind:

'Do everything half as fast and twice as softly as you think you should.'

48

Kissing

An accomplished lover will spend more time on kissing than on any other sexual activity, so you shouldn't just see it as an irritating stop on the way to your ultimate destination.[2] Also, as first impressions count, a good technique could be the difference between going home with a woman and sleeping alone.

The most obvious factor to get right is hygiene. Although it's called 'French' kissing, you shouldn't see this as a signal that it's OK to have a mouth that honks of garlic. In particular, if you smoke and your lover doesn't, you're going to need to supplement the normal round of brushing and gargling with regular mint chewing.

Two other potential problems are excess saliva and clashing teeth. The first can be solved by discreetly swallowing between kisses, or by positioning yourself so that you're lying underneath your partner. The second is best dealt with by refraining from launching yourself at her like a matinée idol each time you kiss, and instead approaching her slowly, with your lips hooding your teeth. There's plenty of time to open your mouth in a sexy Elvis snarl once you're in actual mouth-to-mouth contact.

Lastly, the inexperienced young man should steer clear of 'washing machine kisses', in which you swirl your tongue around deeply, wetly and haphazardly. Messy, graceless, and not half as passionate as you would like to imagine, these will make her feel like she's having her face licked by a long-lost puppy, not a red hot stud. Take note that with kissing, as with dining, good manners are everything, and try these methods out for size . . .

● **Soft kisses:** Just as you wouldn't expect a car to start up and race to sixty on a cold morning, so you shouldn't assume that your lover wants to have her tonsils licked clean without a lengthy preamble. So keep your lips almost closed at first, and kiss her mouth incredibly softly, switching to cover every millimetre of its surface area, with special attention being paid to the corners. Then, keeping your lips as dry as a cocktail party in Jeddah, move them over the contours of her face, lingering on her neck, collar bones, cheeks and ears. If it turns her on — and if she

---

[2] *A bit like Ostend.*

doesn't wear contact lenses — you might take a leaf from F. Scott Fitzgerald, who considered one of his characters 'beautiful enough to be kissed upon the eyes'.

● **Blowing:** As you are moving your mouth over her face, try blowing — again, with infinite subtlety — on her skin. You'll need to have a Colgate 'ring of confidence'[3] in your breath to stop grossing her out, but if you alternate between cold and warm blows, it can have a tantalising effect.

● **Butterfly kisses:** Why limit your kissing by using only your mouth? In this popular method, you flick your eyelashes across her face. Although tricky to do well, and not necessarily doing that much for her, it may make you seem like the last word in sexual sophistication.

● **Lip chew:** When you begin to kiss with open mouths, it's a good idea to gently lick her lower lip with the tip of your tongue, and then 'suck' it into your mouth. When it's trapped between your teeth, gently bite down and twist it, pulling it slightly away from her. Again, the key word here is gentle. (You can also try this with her upper lip, but it's a lot more difficult. And your noses get in the way.)

● **Gum kisses:** This is no walk in the park to do well, and it's best ignored unless you have one of those nice, pointy tongues. It works like this: when you're kissing, bend your tongue tip upwards and run it across her gums where they meet her front teeth. If you get the pressure right, you will send pleasurable tingles across these nerve-endings, which are the most sensitive in the mouth.

● **Jousting tongues:** With your mouths held slightly apart, let the tips of your tongues flicker over each other's surfaces, changing from a back-and-forth to a figure-of-eight motion, and not ignoring the side of her tongue either.

● **Tongue swapping:** As abandoned as it sounds, so wait until you're both warmed up before giving it a whirl. Basically, you take turns to give each other's tongue a blow-job, taking it into your mouth and sucking and slurping along its entire length. You'll be drawn right up against each other when this

---

[3] *This is also the advertising slogan for Preparation H, of course.*

happens, so don't forget to supplement it (and all the techniques mentioned above) with…

● **Using your body:** Great kissing is not just about doing the right things with your mouth. Your hands should also be busy, stroking her neck, squeezing her manfully to you, perhaps even caressing her face and hair (although that *really* annoys some girls). If you're lying down at the time, you can also use your feet to massage the sensitive insides of her calves, or just wrap your legs around hers like a python sizing up a plump goat around dinnertime.[4]

Advanced kissing

As well as these basics, you may want to try some stuff that's not really suitable for the early days of a sexual relationship. Some of these suggestions might seem a little freaky, so it's best to let your lover know what you're intending first …

● **Biting:** Although love bites are something that young teenagers tend to wear with pride, a bit like Blue Peter badges, they are not so much fun if you work in an office where your colleagues will take the piss out of you for a week. So moderate your passion by sucking her skin hard into your mouth rather than trying to take a lump out of it. This will leave a satisfying red mark for the duration of your loveplay, but it'll be gone by the morning. If you *really* can only get your jollies by doing the vampire thing, then try giving her tiny nips instead of proper bites, and avoid parts of her body which will show when she's wearing clothes.

● **Blowbacks:** First popularised over here by hippies on a tight budget, who saw it as an ideal way to make drugs go further. They would take a hit of grass, and then — instead of letting it blow out towards the ceiling — would exhale it into the mouth of a waiting guest. The sexy mouth contact this entailed was clearly too good a thing to waste on straggly-bearded dole-scroungers with a taste for tofu and King Crimson albums, so it was quickly adapted to suit lovers.

---

[4] *Best not to actually describe her legs like this, though.*

If you don't smoke, you can still have some fun transferring substances as varied as ice cubes, sherbet or raw eggs, though it's best to keep them small (to avoid choking) and to make sure you've got some tissues handy to clean up afterwards.

● **Tongue bath:** If you're only kissing her above the neck, then you're not kissing her properly. When she's naked, lie her down and lick her all over, varying between using just the tip of your tongue and its full 'blade'. Keep your tongue wet (but avoid dribbling) and lap away especially at places that don't get much attention in the normal run of things: her palms, the soles of her feet, the crooks of her elbow, her spine and — if she's not wearing foul-tasting deodorant — her armpits. For a finishing touch, point your tongue and lick out her navel.

● **Lipstick trail:** Unless you habitually wear lipstick, this is one that she'll be doing exclusively on you. Get her to put on a generous slathering of 'Scarlet Plush' and then kiss down your chest towards your cock. After each kiss has left a 'target', she then licks or lightly scratches it off. This teasingly delays her progress, allowing you to build up an impressive head of steam.

Massage

Like kissing — and, indeed, much of foreplay — giving a massage is something that many guys think of as an unnecessary detour before the good stuff starts. But, so long as she doesn't expect a full half-hour rub down done to top physiotherapy standards, it can be a good way of turning you both on. You'll get in contact with parts of her body that don't usually see much action, and she'll get the blood pumping to the surface of her skin, making it much easier to turn her on later.

The first thing to get right is preparation, as nothing will kill the mood more than you having to root around your bathroom for the right oils and

accessories. Although a 'dry' massage is fine, it'll be worth your while laying in some lotions (you can get them at most good chemists) because this will make things altogether sloppier and sexier. Supplement these with a massage brush or, at a pinch, a stiff hairbrush, and you'll make the whole job seem more professional. And if you want to really push the boat out, invest in one of those battery-powered massage wands. As well as soothing her muscles with deep vibrations, it'll work magic when applied to her more obviously erogenous zones.

It's also advisable to make sure your sheets are clean before giving a massage, as she'll be itching all night if the sticky oils result in a 'breadcrumb' coating of fluff from your dirty linen. To make sure they stay clean, you can either lay down towels on the bed beforehand, or be even cleverer and use your shower curtain. Simply unhook it and spread it out over the duvet when you're doing the oiling. All you have to do to wash it is hang it up again and take a shower the next morning. Easy.

You should be able to improvise the actual hand techniques yourself, and it's a good rule of thumb that what feels good to you when you're doing it will feel good to her as well. (As long as you make sure that you warm any oils up in your palms before slapping them against her skin.) The only method I can personally recommend is to start with long, light strokes along the length of her back, then gradually make them heavier before softening them again until you're hardly brushing her at all. If you can keep your fingers as light as a spider's legs, she'll find it an electrifying turn on. Wannabe Casanovas can also achieve this effect by brushing her skin with a silk scarf or even feathers — so long as they're the nice, long clean ones, not something you plucked off the Christmas turkey. Or those crappy little brown numbers that leak out of your pillow.

Massage, of course, is a two-way street, so don't deny yourself the pleasure of having one. In fact, hers will probably be better than yours for two reasons. Firstly, if she has long hair, she can use it to brush against your skin like a third hand; and secondly, if she's not too heavy, she can give you a 'Thai' rub. This pleasure, so popular in the brothels of Bangkok that it's practically in the official tourist brochure, is where she coats her entire front with oil, and then gently glides her body all over you. The slurping noises and total skin-to-skin arousal are amazing, but bear in mind that some lotions (e.g. Vaseline and baby oil) can upset the sensitive pH balance inside the vagina, and might end up giving her thrush. Stick to K-Y Jelly, or test out your favourite oils for any nasty side-effects a few days beforehand.

Handwork *Turning You On*

If you're serious about making your love life more exciting, then you need to put extra time aside for it. And this time is best employed warming each other up before you actually begin to fuck. While you probably won't want to attempt all the moves listed below in a single session, you can still use just one or two to make each sexual encounter more memorable. First up, the tricks she can perform for you ...

● **Double hand job:** This one requires a bit of dexterity and rhythm. With you lying on your back, she kneels between your legs and places her right hand round the base of your cock. Her left grips loosely on your helmet. She brings her right hand up, passing it under the left one and off the top of your cock. Then, as her left hand goes down, she moves her right back to the base, where left passes over it. And so on. This is also a lot easier to do if you're well lubed, and once she gets the hang of it, get her to incorporate a slight twisting motion rather than just sticking to a straight up and down.

● **Striptease:** Face it, unless you're one of those male strippers who earns a living by making drunken grannies eat bananas out of their underwear, you're not going to put on a very arousing strip. At best, the sight of you tripping over your trousers and kicking your shoes at the cat is going to give her a good laugh. For women, however, it's a different story — either they're simply better at it, or we're just easier to please. So treat her to some lingerie, stick on a CD, and dim the lights so she's not panicked about any wobbling cellulite. If she's still utterly hopeless, you could do worse than hire a video of the Demi Moore clunker *Striptease* or take her to a lap dancing bar to pick a few tips.

● **Corkscrew hand job:** Frankly, some women aren't much cop at handwork, and they seem to have copied their one boring technique from that Nescafé gesture popularised by Gareth Hunt. However — as everyone wants to be good in bed — she probably won't mind getting some tips, so encourage her to test out a variety of simple alternatives. This one involves her using her grip to travel up and down your cock in a corkscrew motion, and it can be made even more pleasurable if she uses a lubricant like baby oil. (Bear in mind, though,

that this tastes pretty foul, so you'll need to wipe it clean with a towel if you want her to suck you later.) Her spare hand can be used to play with your balls or G-spot, the techniques for which are listed later in this section.

● **Finger-job:** Instead of simply yanking your foreskin up and down, in this method she uses a slight vibrating motion with one hand around the glans. As an added attraction, she also constantly passes her thumb over the wet surface of the helmet, caressing the sensitive nerve-ends.

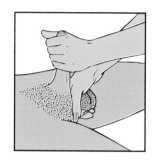

● **Downwards hand job:** A variation on the above, this is supposed to feel as though your cock is constantly entering her pussy. Each of her (well-lubricated) hands takes it in turn to pull downwards on your cock, squeezing around the helmet as it does so. Understandably, this one can hurt if she's not gentle, so make sure she knows your limitations. Especially if you're uncircumsised.

● **Scrotum tickle:** While wanking you off, she can use her spare hand to cup your balls. If she also employs her fingertips to tickle forwards, using a very light touch, the effects on the sensitive skin can be highly arousing.

● **Scratch, smack, squeeze:** Another one that's probably not best attempted with a Torture Garden habitué. She starts off by lightly scratching her sharp nails across the skin of your scrotum. Next, she gently slaps the bag backwards, so that it rocks like a pendulum, and lastly, as you near orgasm, she begins to squeeze your balls while rolling and 'juggling' them in her fingers. This will give you a heightened sense of being 'milked' when you come, and if she masters it your ejaculation will last a few spurts longer.

● **Scrotum tug:** This one's adapted from S&M games, but don't let that put you off — so long as she's gentle, you won't end up with any damage. It works like this: she uses her thumb and forefinger to circle the top of your scrotum, then squeezes them together until your nuts are trapped below. Then, in time with each stroke on your penis, she tugs downwards on your balls, varying the pressure depending on whether your moans are of pleasure or pain. And how much you spent on her birthday present, I dare say.

● **Gloves:** Anything that gives a novel sensation on the skin can only make a hand job better, so don't ignore the possibilities offered by a simple pair of gloves. Although Marigolds may feel a bit too pervy, and mittens too itchy, soft calfskin or suede will set the nerve-ends a-tingle. Even better, get some fur-

55

lined winter gloves and turn them inside out, because you'll never match the softness of these caresses on your balls and shaft.

● **The hair job:** If you don't have any accessories handy, your lover can improvise providing she has very long hair. While leaning down to kiss your balls, she can wrap a thick handful of her locks around your penis (a woven plait is even better), using it to provide a silky friction as she wanks you off. Make sure you give her plenty of warning if you're about to come, however, as semen in her hair is a bore to wash out.

● **The G-spot probe:** As discussed in the 'penis' section earlier in this book (see page 31), correct stimulation of your G-spot can improve an orgasm. So, when you're close to popping your cock, she can slide a well-trimmed — and preferably well-greased — finger an inch or two inside your arse. This is obviously a lot easier if she's positioned near the lower half of your body beforehand.

● **A little bit of 'Spanish':** Why the 'breast wank' should be named after our Andalucian cousins I have no idea, but it is. I don't make the rules up. Anyway, this works best when you're lying side to side and quite close to orgasm, at which point she holds her breasts together, enveloping your penis. You then help out by thrusting away. Clearly, this works best if she has large boobs, and a spot of baby oil won't go amiss either. If she's lucky enough to have boobs that hang quite close together, she can even lie you on your back and brush them around your cock from above. Personally, I've only met one woman who could do this all the way to orgasm without using her hands, but it was amazing so I recommend at least giving it a try.

● **Genuphallation:** Now this is a weird one: she slaps plenty of oil into the 'valley' behind her knee, and closes her leg up until the calf and thigh are tight and parallel. This provides a mock vagina for you to enter. Having tried it, I can only say it's a bit bony on the cock, but it might work well if your beloved is particularly lardy in the pins area.

● **Bagpiping:** Although just as freaky as genuphallation, this one at least offers her the chance of some pleasure as well. The armpit is an erogenous zone, and if hers is well-lubed, you can make love to it. She closes her arm shut once your cock is inside, and you thrust in and out, possibly withdrawing to ejaculate on her breasts when you feel close to climax. Make sure she's shaved recently, however, or the stubble could play havoc with the fragile skin of your glans.

Handwork *Turning Her On*

Now it's her turn. Again, bear in mind that no woman will want to experience all these moves in one session, so ration them out until you know which ones are guaranteed to get her smokin', and which ones simply don't hit the right spot. It will really help you to learn how to give her pleasure if she allows you to watch her masturbate, but if she's shy about this there's a useful compromise. When you start to touch her pussy before sex, just keep your finger still and get her to grind and wriggle against it. This will give you a good idea of the target area, and also clue you in to how hard or soft she likes to be caressed. Once again, and in an even bigger type size, I emphasize:

'Do everything half as fast and twice as softly as you think you should.'

● **The warm-up:** After you've treated the rest of her body to foreplay, begin to stroke her thighs, letting your hand trail softly up one and then down the other, pausing only momentarily over the pussy. Then make each stroke shorter, so you're beginning to zone in on her vagina. Let your fingers teasingly caress the really smooth skin of her upper, inner thighs, and then finally run one finger up and down the crease formed by the labia. Don't attempt to penetrate her yet: just glide gently over the outside.

● **Kneading:** Place two fingers along the length of her labia, and use a soft kneading motion to stimulate her. You can move your fingers slowly all the way from the mons pubis to the perineum while doing this. If she's still dry after a few minutes, lick your fingertips and run them on the inside edge of the labia, but — again — don't try to touch her clitoris or get inside her yet.

● **The pubic pull:** Place the heel of your hand on the skin just above her pubes. Lock a few hairs in between your fingers and gently pull them in a swirling motion, taking care to cause pleasure not discomfort. You can simultaneously use your middle fingertip to touch her pussy.

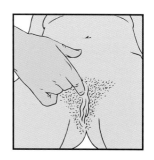

● **Making circles:** When her pussy begins to open up, dip your finger slowly inside to moisten it with the natural glandular lubrication. Then rub this fluid around the clitoral area, avoiding direct contact with the clitoris itself, and instead making small circles or figures of eight around the base or hood.

● **The pop out:** Using two fingers held closed together, make small, delicate circles over the clitoris. Then place the fingertips on either side of it and press them in towards her body, making clitoris 'pop' out. You can then use your other hand to caress it.

● **Cupping:** Placing your palm over her pubic hair, bend your middle finger so it's angled to touch her clitoris. While applying gentle downward pressure with the heel of your hand, use your finger to rub her clitoris up and down, in circles, or to strum it subtly like a guitar string. If you keep the two fingers next to it straight, they can caress the edges of her labia.

● **Spoons foreplay:** You don't even need hands to do this one, but she will need to be very wet. Simply lie behind her in the 'spoons' position (see page 115) and slide your cock between her thighs. Without penetrating her pussy, let the head of shaft of your cock rub against her clitoris. She can set the speed and pressure to suit her, so all you really have to do is massage her breasts and kiss her neck while she's getting busy. It's very easy for you to come in this way, but try to make sure she's climaxed first or it will be agonising on your glans. Oh, and there's a slight risk she might get pregnant if she carries on rubbing once you've come, so make sure she knows, eh?

● **Scissors:** Place two fingers all the way inside her pussy, then open and close them like a pair of scissors. You can do this either vertically or horizontally, but make sure's she's very turned on or the stretching feeling may hurt her. As will your fingernails unless they're well manicured.

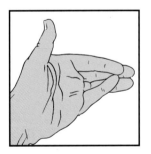

● **The pistol:** Close the four fingers of one hand into a point, keeping the thumb up at right angles so that the whole thing resembles a cocked pistol. Use the ball of the thumb to stroke her clitoris while you plunge the fingers in and out of her pussy. Try to adopt a twisting motion as well as an in-out one, and, naturally, ensure she's wet enough to take this bantamweight version of 'fisting'.

● **The dipped finger:** Alternate dipping a finger into her wet pussy and slowly sliding it out of her in an upwards direction. As it heads towards her navel, it's entire length will roll against her clitoris, and — if you care to keep up the rhythm of this sawing motion — it's a good way to ensure she comes.

● **The trident:** Put your thumb against her clitoris, slide your first three fingers

inside her pussy, and use your outstretched little finger to caress her perineum or anus. Many women rate this, as you're managing to stimulate her in three different ways at once, but unless you've got hands like Pat Jennings, I'm afraid your knuckle joints start to ache after a while.

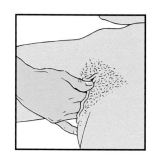

● **Vibrators and dildos:** Individual models are rated and reviewed on page 147, but if you do use them in your love play, bear in mind that most girls don't actually insert a vibrator when they use it, preferring to let it hover over their clitoris. As for dildos, don't be afraid to use any handy household objects so long as they are clean, safe and she's OK with them. And don't assume they have to be huge: as well as making your penis look smaller, objects the size of cucumbers will require lashings of artificial lubricant. (Anyway, most girls I know swear by a bottle of Mum roll-on deodorant for this purpose, and they are only about 4 inches long.)

A relaxed woman is less likely to feel nervous or uptight, so the best way to ensure you can bring her off with just your fingers is to tell her she's got all the time in the world. And mean it. And, while it's great to show what a virtuoso you are with different techniques, remember that once she nears the 'home straight', you should stick to a steady rhythm and just one method. Stopping and starting something new is only going to set her back a few minutes. Be aware also that her 'ideal point of pressure' can change from hour to hour, so don't assume that what worked last time will necessarily work again. Lastly, if she's experiencing real trouble in coming, she can help by clenching and unclenching her buttock and vaginal muscles, and sometimes just by pressing the soles of her feet together.

Oral Sex *Blow Jobs*

Forget black and white. Forget Christian or Muslim. In reality, the world is divided into just two types of men: those who love getting blow jobs, and those who are dead. The most remarkable thing about this state of affairs is, of course, that so many women are lousy at giving head. Sure, they'll put their lips around your cock, and they may even bob up and down a bit without making it seem like they're doing you the world's biggest favour, but that's not the same

as getting it right. When it comes to the crunch, all too many perform like a drunk in a pub suddenly handed the karaoke microphone — ten out of ten for trying, love, but don't give up your day job.[5]

Mind you, when it comes to girls being amateur at oral sex, we're not entirely blameless ourselves. Nearly every man will tell his lover 'That was fantastic!' after a blow job, even if it was crap. Why do we say this? Easy: to protect her ego so she's prepared to try again next time, because the fact remains that even a bad blow job is pretty good. The mouth is the most versatile of all the sexual apertures, with a ready supply of free lubrication and a wide selection of moving parts. In short, it's a pussy with brains, a vagina de luxe. Employed with intelligence and verve, it should be capable of not just taking a man to heaven and back on a regular basis, but of actually introducing him to God. All this only makes it more tragic that so many women are unsure how to use it properly.

But you don't have to put up with that any more. If you're prepared to make an effort by learning some of the moves in this book, then so should she. And you could do a lot worse than leave this section open on her bedside table . . .

● **Preparation:** Clearly, hygiene is incredibly important here. But, as it may surprise you to learn that her mouth is home to far more germs than your old fella, it isn't just a matter of you giving your tackle a once over with Imperial Leather. No, she should also make sure she's had a good brush and floss too. And, as watching her mouth work on your penis is always much more fun that simply viewing the back of her head, you should make sure she's positioned in such a way that gives you panoramic views of the whole business. Get her to tuck her hair behind her ear, or hold it there yourself, and make use of any mirrors to provide alternative visuals. As for technique, even if she's experienced she may require some practical assistance on exactly how hard, lively and fast *you* prefer to be fellated, so I'd recommend that you demonstrate by sucking on her thumb beforehand.

● **Basic blow jobs:** If she's nervous about giving head, which usually happens if she thinks she might choke, then get her to keep one hand gripped around the bottom of your shaft, and don't do any thrusting yourself. Once she's happy, she should make an 'O' with her lips, keeping her teeth well away from the action, and simply slide up and down, using her tongue to keep your penis

---

[5] *Unless you work in the White House, in which case hang on for the publishing opportunity.*

wet. The act of licking saliva onto your shaft for this purpose should naturally provide enough swirling stimulation to make you come. But to make things more sensational, ask her to experiment with . . .

● **The hand up:** Instead of simply holding one hand around the base of your penis, get her to lift it up and down in rhythm with her mouth. She can either tug it in the opposite direction to her lips — taking care not to stretch your skin too far — or do it in tandem with her lips, thus giving you a simultaneous hand and blow job. One refinement on this is for her to drag her hand all the way up your cock with each stroke, so that her mouth is 'forced' off the top, and her wrapped fingers (of which only the little one will still be curled around your glans) form a 'cup' above your cock. As the blow job continues, this cup will gradually get filled with saliva, making the downstrokes sexily lubricated. Oh, and it also makes your cock appear to be 3 inches bigger if you're watching.

● **The harmonica:** A good blow job shouldn't just concentrate on your helmet area, so she can alternate work up there with some other goodies. This one involves turning her head parallel to your shaft, and pressing her lips softly around it as though playing the harmonica. If she makes very soft nips with her teeth and runs her tongue dartingly along the length, it provides a nice 'secondary' sensation, useful for delaying your orgasm without actually stopping oral sex.

● **The banjo tickle:** Another good one for her to switch to if she wants to stop you coming just yet. Here she uses the tip of her tongue to strum on your frenulum, that little thread of skin stretching from your jap's eye. Her touch should be light, keeping her pointed tongue far from her teeth, as this is a very fragile part of the body. Some men find this a real turn on, others say it does nothing for them. But, hey, it's only going to take you five seconds to find out.

● **The pastry blow job:** Using the 'pastry roll' technique already described in the 'Masturbation' section (see page 42), she rubs your shaft between her open hands, curling her tongue and lips around the glans. As you'll take longer to come this way, it's best kept for interesting 'warm up' work at the beginning of a blow job, with her switching to something more definitively up and down when you want to climax.

● **The hum job:** A unique variation which works just as well on the balls as the penis, here she presses her closed lips against you and hums. On the plus side,

this sends tiny vibrations through your genitals, making it great for summoning up an erection when you think you're too tired to screw. On the minus side, she has to be careful not to hum too hard, as this will result in extremely unerotic farting noises.

● **Ball sucking:** One of the things that makes a blow job great is if she shows a lot of all round, cock-worshipping enthusiasm, rather than primly bobbing up and down. One index of this gusto is the attention she pays to your balls and anus as well as just your penis. So, while her fingers are toying with your perineum or G-spot, she can use her mouth to take one or both of your balls into her mouth, sucking them and curling her tongue over them. Indeed, if she doesn't like swallowing, this is a great alternative for a memorable climax — at the point of no return, she switches her mouth from your glans to your scrotum, and wanks you off with her hand.

● **Carrying on:** One of the main things women get wrong about oral sex is stopping their motion as soon as you start to come. However, as orgasm and ejaculation are not always simultaneous (and it *is* possible to have one without the other), she would do well to carry on sucking you for at least fifteen seconds after you've shot your bolt.

● **Swallowing:** If your girlfriend is a 'spitter', there are a few steps you can take to persuade her that semen is OK to swallow. Firstly, when you come she can take your cock deep into her mouth, because the back of the tongue has far fewer tastebuds than the front. Secondly, you can tell her to put your cock *under* her tongue when you climax, as this will swill most of the offending spunk away from her tastebuds. And lastly, you might try the perversion known as 'snowballing', in which she kisses your semen back into your mouth and *you* swallow it. Do this often enough without throwing up, and she might start to believe you when you say it tastes fine.

By the way, if she pleads 'calories' as an excuse for not swallowing, inform her that the average ejaculation contains less than 150 kilojoules of energy, so it's unlikely to turn her into a circus fatwoman.[6]

● **Coming on her:** Rather than just coming onto the sheets or into a tissue, you can finish off by ejaculating on her breasts and neck (known, for obvious

---

[6] *I apologise to the Union of Circus Fatwomen if that is indeed the reason their members got so ridiculously fat.*

reasons, as a 'pearl necklace'), or into her face (known as a 'facial'). Although it's a lie to say 'semen is good for your skin', it won't do her any harm either, and few things are as dirtily sexy as a woman rubbing your come into her skin after sex.

● **Deep throat:** Although a common enough sight in porno movies, this is actually no cinch to pull off. (If you want to know just how tricky it is, try putting a cucumber in your mouth and see how far you get before choking.) Nevertheless, because it's such a visual turn-on, here are some pointers for your lover. Firstly, she should tilt her chin so that her mouth and throat are in a straight line. Secondly, she should try to breathe on the 'outstroke'. Thirdly, if she feels like gagging, a quick gulping swallow will help alleviate the situation. The best position for deep throat is for her to lie on your stomach facing your toes, but as this means you won't see anything, make sure you've moved that big bedroom mirror first, eh?

● **Milking:** A few seconds after you've come, the ultra-keen fellatrix may be able to squeeze even more semen out of you. This works in two ways: she can either delicately pinch a finger and thumb around the neck of your penis and 'milk' it out, or she can combine this with lightly tugging your scrotum forwards. The amount of spunk produced will only be small, but if she laps it off with a pointed tongue, it makes for a very appealing sight.

Food and Oral Sex

Oral sex can be even more enlivened by adding food and drink to the process. Here are some favourites, listed with the effects they have ...

Crème de Menthe: A popular twist on offer at high-class brothels is the famous Crème de Menthe blow job. Your lover takes a teaspoonful of this revolting peppermint liqueur onto her tongue, then lets it dribble all over your cock. For a short moment you'll look unsettlingly like the Incredible Hulk, but then the fun begins: the alcohol will begin to 'burn' your skin, and she alternates this feeling by blowing on it, giving a kinky mix of hot and cold. Soon your cock starts to feel deliciously numb, at which point she switches to

normal blow job mode. If you're on a budget, strikingly similar effects can be achieved with minty mouthwash, or even if she just sucks an extra strong mint.

Cinnamon oil: As well as making your penis taste nicer, a few dabs of this spice oil (available in herbalists and places like the Body Shop) will make your cock feel as though it's itching and on fire. Needless to say, this feeling recedes as she sucks it dry.

Again, if you're on a budget, you could always try using sherbet — though it's not as effective.

Tea: A real favourite with blow-job fans, and thus a possible explanation why those PG Tips chimpanzees were always so fucking cheerful. She takes a mouthful of Earl Grey, having let it cool in the cup for about five minutes after boiling, and envelopes your penis, being careful not to spill any. (The best position is with her on her knees in front of you, as this keeps her mouth roughly horizontal.) The warmth you get from this adds a great bonus to a blow job, and — so long as she can keep the tea in her chops — probably makes your semen easier to swallow too.

Ice: Brilliant when alternated with tea, as it moves you from one extreme of temperature to another, but no slouch on its own either. She sucks on a small cube (not too big in case she chokes) and glides it artfully around your bell end while she sucks. This one can be done anywhere and at any angle — ice doesn't stain upholstery.

Yoghurt: If she's shy about giving you oral sex, this can turn it into a friendly game. You simply lob on some yoghurt (make sure it's near room temperature though, or else your cock will shrink with cold) and then she licks it off. Some women, presumably the ones who starred at Home Economics, may be tempted to take this too far, however, leading to humiliating 'cake display' incidents in which the yoghurt layer is decorated with strawberries or vermicelli. If you fear this might be the case, substitute it with taramasalata. Nothing 'goes' with that.

Champagne: Although not quite what Dom Pérignon had in mind when he invented champagne in his monastery, this works pretty well. She takes a mouthful of fizz and lets the bubbles stimulate you while she performs. Don't think you can save money by using 7 Up or Coca-Cola, however, as these contain acids which will sting the urethra.

Cunnilingus

A damned ugly word, cunnilingus (from *cunnus*, the vulva, and *lingus*, the tongue) is also a damned difficult thing to do well. For a start, vaginas are tricky things to navigate. When you consider that a clitoris can be as small as a grain of rice, and that it's concealed beneath a jungle of pubic hair and two folds of flesh, it's no surprise that so many men just lap away haphazardly, like a blind man ducking for apples. What makes matters worse is that women rarely offer assistance. Perhaps out of politeness, gratitude, or just plain insecurity about the appearance of their genitals — once memorably categorised by Martin Amis as varying between 'the greasy waistcoat pocket and the slashed vole's stomach'[7] — they are reluctant to bark out the sort of Golden Shot style instructions we'd be happy to hear. Nevertheless, if you try out these tips on your girlfriend, I guarantee she'll soon be dragging you upstairs come bedtime.

● **Preparation:** A lot of men muff-dive for the wrong reason — because it's the quickest way to get their lover wet enough to penetrate. If this is your attitude, change it. For cunnilingus to work best on her, she has to know that a) you love doing it, and b) she's got all the time in the world. (Get her in this state of mind, of course, and she'll actually climax *faster*, because she won't be tense.) So, don't treat it as a chore or a race, make sure you pay proper attention to the rest of foreplay first, and when you do begin to lick her pussy, don't dive straight for the clitoris. The key word is 'lingering'.

Also, as many women worry about the flavour of their vagina, put her at ease with a comment like 'I love the way you taste' or even a simple 'mmmm' of pleasure. Above all, don't ignore the other parts of her body just because you're giving her head, and try not to leave her in the cold by taking all the duvet down there with you. Once you've got these points straight, prepare for any problems you might face, such as . . .

● **She tastes bad:** No matter how thorough she is with the old Camay, a woman's pussy will retain a unique musky aroma. Most people like it, but if you don't it could be because you fall into a group known to scientists as 'supertasters'. Basically, this means you have a higher concentration of tastebuds on your tongue (as many as 1100 per square centimetre), and if this is indeed the case, then you probably find things like coffee and curry

---

[7] And I bet the Hallmark card company are looking forward to his first book of love poems.

unpalatable too. As many as 10 per cent of men suffer from this condition, and there are really only two things you can do about it. The first is to numb your tongue with an ice cube before cunnilingus (don't try using a chilli pepper — it may be a more effective local anaesthetic, but it will make her howl in pain), and the second is to put a substance with a powerful, pleasant flavour on her clitoris. Perhaps the most democratic choice would be sherbet: not only will this mask the natural womanly taste you dislike so much, but it will also give her a saucy tingle as it begins to froth up.

Alternatively, it could simply be that she's no gangbuster on the hygiene front, in which case secretions that form under the hood of her clitoris (similar to smegma) will give off an unpleasant odour. It's a tough thing to mention, of course, so your best bet is to lick it away. This will only take a few seconds, and after that it should be plain sailing, tastewise.

● **Jaw ache:** Cunnilingus can be a tiring business, and there's a good chance you'll begin to feel cramp in your jaw or tongue. If this happens, try keeping your mouth still and making the movements just with your neck, or get her to grind her pussy against you while you take a break.

● **Stubble:** The George Michael look may go down well with the girls in a club,[8] but on the soft skin of their faces, thighs and pussy it's often less popular. If you rub against her too harshly or for too long, she may get a minor rash that'll be painful for a day or so. If this is a real dilemma, then try softening your bristles before bedtime, either with a shaving balm or normal shampoo.

● **Clumsy tongue:** If, like me, you have a 'digestive biscuit tongue' rather than a pointy one like that bloke out of Kiss, then cunnilingus can feel rather hit and miss. One good way of practising your agility is to get one of those small silver iced balls they decorate cakes with and put it deep in the teeth of a hairbrush. As your tongue gets more nimble, you'll soon be able to lap it out within seconds. And once you're able to lick it away to nothing like a gobstopper while it's still wedged at the base of the brush, then, Grasshopper, you'll be ready to treat any girl to a virtuoso performance.

● **How do I know she likes it?** Trust me, you could get long odds at Ladbroke's on her *not* enjoying oral sex. But if you're worried that she's

---

[8] *Well, better than with the LAPD anyway.*

not getting turned on, try this easy experiment. If her erect clitoris begins to shrink and retract during muff diving, then you're doing something wrong. Either switch to handwork, or ask her how she would prefer you to lick her out.

● **Pubic hair:** A perennial hazard of muff-diving is that a pubic hair will find its way onto your tongue. But instead of noisily trying to cough it up like a cat with a furball, make an effort to be discreet. Either pause for a moment to pick it off with your fingers, or lick it off against her thigh. Do this smoothly and she won't even know there was a problem. And now let's move on to the actual techniques...

● **Basic cunnilingus:** This is your bread-and-butter muff-diving, but it's none the less effective for that. Start by kissing her labia majora softly, using only your lips, as though kissing someone hello at a party, and then probe your tongue into her labia minora as she begins to wetten. Move up to the clitoris, but kiss *around* it rather than straight onto it. Use your fingers in any of the ways described earlier in the 'Hand Work' section (see page 57). Lick it gently, using a combination of circular or up-and-down motions, sticking to just one as she approaches climax. It's fine to change the rhythm at the start, but keep it regular once she nears the finishing line (or the chances are she'll never get there). As for the pressure, it's a personal choice, and one you should let her make. If she presses her pussy hard into your face, she probably wants it stronger, and vice versa.

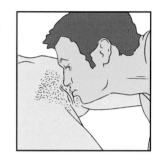

● **Nibbling:** Although her pussy should be treated with the same respect you afford your cock, you can try a little light nibbling with your teeth during oral sex. Keep it very gentle and stick to the labia. *Do not*, under any circumstances, bite her clitoris.

● **Tongue fucking:** Nicely filthy, and thus a turn-on for both of you, this is where you penetrate her vagina with your tongue. You can either jab it in and out like a woodpecker, or swirl it around inside the first centimetre of pussy. As you do this *very* French kiss, your lips will naturally caress up against her labia, increasing her delight.

● **Blowing:** Some women respond very well to soft blowing on their pussy and, especially, their clitoris, so long as you do it subtly rather than like someone trying to get a fire going in the wilderness. Be careful, however, to

keep your breath on the outside of her: if you actually blow *up* her vagina, it can cause a fatal embolism. And I bet she's going to let you try *this* one now.

● **The 69:** No foreplay technique has achieved quite such a legendary status as the 'soixante-neuf' — which is surprising, as it's not particularly satisfying. Sure it's intimate, sure it's democratic, but it's hard for her to concentrate on coming herself if she's worried about sucking you off, and you yourself are at a poor angle to lick her clitoris. Personally, I think it's wiser to stick to the 'onze' or '11', a position where you lie parallel but take it strictly in turns to pleasure each other.

● **Eating in:** In many ways, her pussy is even more convenient to eat from than your penis, and inserting various items of food and drink will certainly add novelty to the proceedings. The most favoured menu items are strawberries and grapes, though I have heard great things about Mars Bars and Crunchies (which, according to my female source 'fizz like crazy inside me'.) An ice cube, warmed up on the skin of her back to take the frost off first, is also a winner, with 'tea blowbacks' — so long as it's not too hot, of course — attracting some interest from the judging panel.

● **The Scrabble lick:** This one was told to me by a guy I know, who suggests that in the early stages of cunnilingus, when you've yet to settle into a rhythm, it can help to stave off boredom if you play a little game with your lover. Use your tongue to spell out letters on her clitoris, and see whether she is sensitive enough to decode them. Brilliant? Absurd? Well, I dare say Carol Vorderman would enjoy it anyway.

● **Face sitting:** If she has the slightest dominatrix instinct, she'll certainly get off on this one. Just lie back on the bed, and let her squat over your head, lowering her pussy until it's above your mouth. In this position she is totally in charge of how hard and where she wants your tongue to be, so it's very good for you too from an educational point of view.

● **The orgasm suck:** When you sense that she is beginning to come, try sucking her clitoris into your lips and holding it there. This will intensify her feelings of orgasm, but make sure you're ready to release it if she gets too sensitive to be touched after her climax.

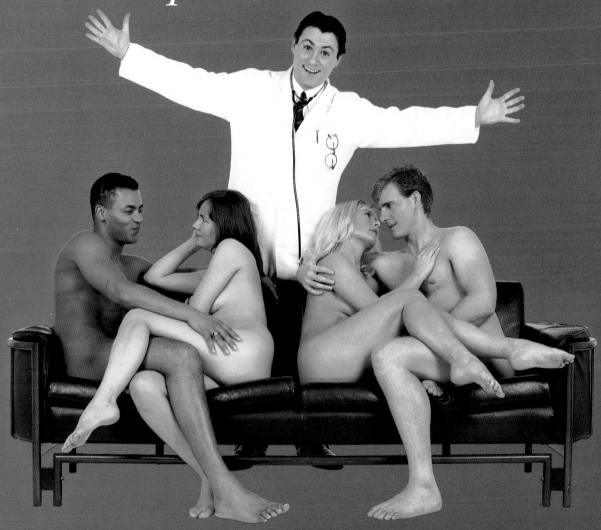

CHAPTER 4 *positions*

Once you have mastered the art of foreplay, it's time to look at the many different ways there are of making love. Naturally, I am not the first hack to see a lucrative publishing opportunity in this subject, so it seems only right that I should begin by tipping my cap to the experts who blazed the trail.

Most worthy of praise is a fellow named Vatsyayana, who lived in India around the year AD400, and who wrote the most famous ever book on sexual positions: the *Kama Sutra*[1]. In truth, his book is not only concerned with sex — it also contains chapters about religious well-being, good manners and (I kid you not) teaching starlings how to speak — but, let's face it, if it weren't for the pictures of naked couples entwining their sweaty bodies, it would probably have gone out of print in about, oh, AD401. Also of great value are two medieval works of Arabian origin, the *Ananga Ranga* by Kalyana Malla, and *The Perfumed Garden* by Sheikh Nefzawi. Reading them, and noting the sheer freight of scholarly detail they put into the study of sex, one can't help thinking that Arabs in the Middle Ages had *way* too much time on their hands. I mean, if they'd devoted a similar amount of energy to, say, science projects, then they'd have been manufacturing digital watches and F-16 fighter planes while the rest of us European guys were still going, 'Wow! Check it out! That hut's got wattle *and* daub!'

Despite the efforts of these gentlemen, however, most of us still only use three basic positions when we're making love. Of course, they're great and they do the job, but if you want a long relationship to stay exciting it's best to know some extra moves. I've divided these into five main groups: man on top, girl on top, rear entry, side by side and complex. Many of them appear in the aforementioned works, but I have made two important changes for present day readers. Firstly, instead of using the original names such as 'The Splitting of a Bamboo' and 'The Mating of the Frog', I have given them modern titles. And secondly, although the couples representing them in the photographs are young, slim and attractive, I have also recommended some handy tips for people who are shorter, fatter and uglier than the sort of models who earn their living by simulating sex in illustrated books of an adult nature.

Next we come to the question of when and how to try them out. As many of them require a good deal of forethought, co-ordination and practice to get your limbs in the right position, it's best not to spring them on a girlfriend unawares. Perhaps the best solution is to learn them together beforehand, but even then I

---

[1] *He told his wife it was about elephants.*

would recommend moderation. A change in positions should come naturally, and if you start barking out instructions like 'Number 43! Then two minutes of number 17!' she's going to feel like an over-worked waitress in the Golden Pagoda. If you forget a detail or two once you're on the job, compromise rather than break things off to refer to this book. While keeping it handy under the pillow, or even propped open on a music stand is undoubtedly practical, it's not conducive to great romance.[2]

Above all, know your limitations. Although new positions may help you both find a different kind of bliss, and pausing to adopt each new variation will help you delay ejaculation naturally, without having to think about long division problems, they do require a certain level of fitness. I can still vividly recall my own attempt at The Toilet Seat position (page 126), which ended with my flabby, unathletic frame being crushed into a pretzel shape, and my lower back being so badly ricked that I half expected a visit and kindly handshake from Jimmy Saville the next morning.

But enough bad news. There are bound to be some new delights for you in the fifty-odd pages which follow. So enjoy...

[2]*And there's good chance that your girlfriend will say, like my proofreader did, 'Hey, you stole that music stand idea from a Frank Skinner routine.'*

RATINGS

Like Egon Ronay, I have awarded a rating to each of the positions described in this book. The four categories I've chosen concern the suitability of each variation for men who are:

Shorter than their partner

Unimpressively hung

Well hung

Overweight

They work as follows:

1 = Totally Unsuitable
2 = Not Much Cop
3 = Average
4 = Good
5 = Excellent

71

MAN ON TOP *positions*

Most people associate this style with boring sex, probably because it was the position officially sanctioned by Victorian missionaries. When these worthies arrived to convert Africa, they were horrified to find that the natives were accustomed to shagging in every posture under the sun, often going so far as to enjoy themselves. Quick to pounce on any activity more pleasurable than singing 'Kum Ba Yah' in the round, they insisted that everyone stick to the so-called 'missionary position', a technique in which the man does press ups while the woman lies underneath him pretending to be dead. Now, liberal commentators might be tempted to speculate, in a smart-arsed *Guardian*-reading way, who were really the 'uncivilised' ones here. But not me. Mainly because the Africans also worshipped raccoons.

However, the point is that man on top positions don't have to be dull. Indeed, they have many good points to recommend them. It's easier to control your rate of thrust (and thus your orgasm) for instance, and it leaves her hands free so she can use them to caress your back or play with your anus. On the minus side, some of them are pretty hard work on the arm muscles, it's difficult to use your fingers to stimulate her clitoris while doing them, and most of them result in relatively shallow penetration. Nevertheless, remember the wisdom of the phrase 'nothing ventured, nothing gained', and give these a crack. Not all of them are startlingly different from each other, but sometimes even the slightest change can add a slice of novelty to your routine . . .

POSITION 1 *The Foot Stroke*

How to do it: She lies on her back underneath you, with her legs quite widely open and her feet hooked between your legs.

Good points: This differs from straight missionary sex because the woman uses her feet to push up and down along your thighs, setting a rhythm and gently scratching you with her toenails. Also, as both your bodies are pretty much constantly pressing against each other, there is excellent skin-to-skin stimulation.

Bad points: Not particularly flattering unless you're both in tip-top physical shape. Your gut will hang down, and her breasts, if not extremely firm, will flop to the side. (Mind you, a good suggestion if she's self-conscious about this, is for her to keep her upper arms pressed into her ribs, as this will perk her breasts up to a near-silicone standard of firmness.)

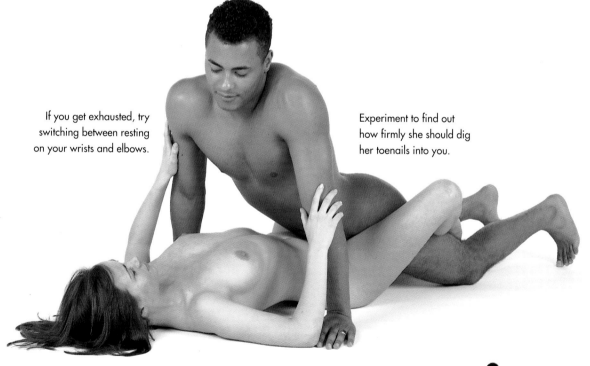

If you get exhausted, try switching between resting on your wrists and elbows.

Experiment to find out how firmly she should dig her toenails into you.

POSITION 2 *Crossed Feet*

RATINGS

How to do it: You keep yourself raised high above her, entering her vagina quite steeply, while she crosses her ankles over your bum or back.

Good points: She can pull you inside her, thus giving her control of the pace and rhythm. Also, because she has her thighs lifted, you will get a better angle for deeper penetration, and be more likely to rub against her clitoris.

Bad points: You have to stay up on your wrists most of the time.

Her legs dictate the desired speed of your thrusts, which is especially arousing as she approaches orgasm.

If you begin to tire, she can help support you with her hands.

POSITION 3 *Meeting Halfway*

How to do it: Keeping yourself elevated on hands and knees, you let her lift her pelvis from the bed. You then do 'half thrusts' each in mid-air.

Good points: In this position the woman can buck against you, meeting you stroke for stroke. This gives a nicely abandoned, animal feel to the proceedings. (If you want to see it done well, watch the famous opening bonk scene in the movie *Betty Blue*.)

Bad points: If you have a short penis, you're likely to 'slip out' quite a lot. And if you mistime your thrusts, you could get a painful knock on the end of your old fella.

If she keeps her hands on your arse, there's less chance of you losing the rhythm.

For maximum appeal, keep the rest of your bodies from touching.

POSITION 4 *The L-Shape*

RATINGS

How to do it: You squat back on your calves and, gripping her by the waist or hips, softly pull her body towards you on each stroke.

Good points: Visually very appealing, as your partner is all stretched out below you. It's easy to lean forwards and stroke her breasts or stomach, and similarly to have her suck on your fingers while you screw.

Bad points: Shallow penetration, not much ease of movement, and it's bloody impossible to kiss unless she has the abdominal muscles of a trained gymnast.

Use pillows to raise her back to a convenient height before starting.

Gently pull her towards you to help each movement.

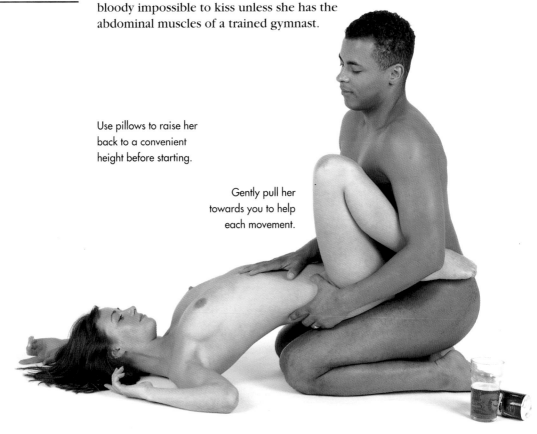

POSITION 5 *The Press*

RATINGS

How to do it: Simple. Just lie on top of her, and get her to slide her legs over yours so she has some purchase for thrusting.

Good points: Extremely intimate, as your entire bodies — from head to toe — are touching.

Bad points: Shallow penetration. Severely restricted range of movement. And a very real chance you may squash her, so don't even dream about it unless you are a) well hung, and b) tipping the scales well under the light-welterweight limit.

Excellent opportunities for kissing her neck.

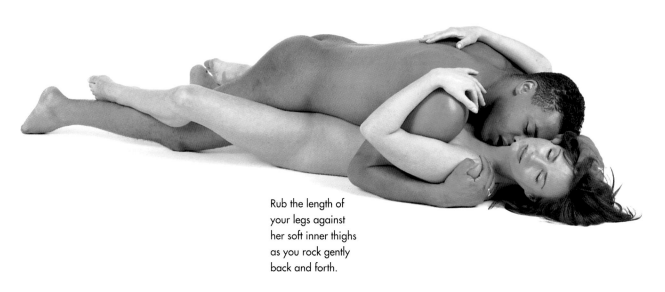

Rub the length of your legs against her soft inner thighs as you rock gently back and forth.

POSITION 6 *Grip the Headboard*

RATINGS

How to do it: Go to the top end of the bed and hold yourself in place with your hands. Grip on the sheets with your toes for extra hold.

Good points: Gives you excellent leverage and is less exhausting than most man on top positions. You can even free up one hand for caressing her breasts.

Bad points: Useless if you sleep on a futon.

Good grip allows for firm, deep penetration.

Her hands are free to stroke or scratch your back.

78

POSITION 7 *The Lotus Position*

How to do it: Kneel on all fours above her, and carefully help her cross her legs into the Lotus position. Always make sure she is comfortable, especially when you start to lie some of your weight across her.

Good points: Extremely unusual and inventive, so it's unlikely you'll have done it with too many other women. Gives a slight whiff of bondage, which may be a turn-on for you or your partner.

Bad points: She must be very supple to manage this position, so don't attempt it with anyone who flunked yoga class. Also, as her legs will be pushing your body up and away from her, you need to have a long cock to get anywhere.

She can rock back and forth, but her movements will be more restricted than normal.

You can easily reach down and stroke the sensitive soles of her feet.

POSITION 8 *Foot on Chest*

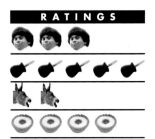

How to do it: Like the next three positions, this is a variation in which the woman uses her legs and feet to help you rock back and forth. In this version, you squat back on your calves, and she supports herself by resting one outstretched leg on your thigh. The other leg is bent so that the foot pushes into your chest.

Good points: It's ideal if she gets her jollies from a toe job, as you can administer one while fucking her, instead of just keeping it for foreplay. Plus, the folded pose effectively constricts her vagina, so it's a good option for guys with short penises.

Bad points: She can't do much with her hands, and her knee will inevitably cover one of her breasts. Even if she's thinner than Kate Moss, the bending of her torso may make her feel that she looks fat. Also, it's a bugger to untangle if you suddenly need to answer the phone.

Given the precarious nature of this position, it's best to vary in-and-out thrusts with figures of eight.

Make sure she's washed her feet. Obviously.

POSITION 9 *The Deckchair*

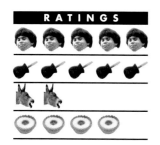

How to do it: She lies on her back, with both her legs curled back onto her chest. She rests the soles of her feet against your chest, while you bend your body so you are fucking 'downwards'.

Good points: Very deep penetration, so it's perfect for the less well-hung. It's also easy to fondle her arse and to reach between her legs to stimulate her clitoris. Plus, it's worth noting that this position will 'tense' the muscles of her vagina, helping her build up towards orgasm.

Bad points: It's possible to hurt her by thrusting too hard, so you have to go slowly and carefully. It's probably not the best position to finish off in, especially if you get really carried away when you come. Also, a real no-no if you prefer to get your rocks off when looking at her breasts.

Prop her bum up on some pillows to make this feel like less of a workout.

She can grip and knead your buttocks to give extra pleasure.

POSITION 10 *The Legover*

How to do it: The woman lies slightly on her side, twisting so that her right leg goes over your left shoulder, or vice versa. It's essential to prop her up with pillows so that her pussy is at the right height for penetration.

Good points: Your balls can rub against the soft skin of her thighs as you move in and out, and — visually, at least — you get the best of both worlds, being able to see her tits and arse cheeks.

Bad points: Unless she fancies a trip to the leg fractures ward of your local hospital, it's impossible to kiss her. Plus, penetration will not be deep, especially if you have a gut.

Both hands are free to caress her body.

You can maintain a rhythmic scratching of her thigh in time with each stroke.

POSITION 11 *The Double Legover*

How to do it: As with number 10, except she puts both her legs over one of your shoulders. Oddly enough, this makes manoeuvring much easier, so you should get a more active romp.

Good points: Very deep penetration. Allows you to stroke the backs of her thighs and calves, and to kiss her feet during the action.

Bad points: Uncomfortable if she's not very lithe or gymnastic. Plus it's almost impossible to stimulate her clitoris like this, so make sure that she's well warmed up beforehand.

It's easy to change from vaginal to anal sex without any fussing about.

If her knees are kept pressed together, this will 'tighten' the vagina, causing extra friction on your cock. And thus more pleasure.

POSITION 12 *The Knees Up*

RATINGS

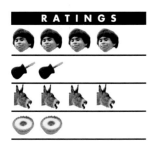

How to do it: The woman rests her feet on her partner's hips, giving her some purchase to thrust back at him during sex. He arches his back and uses short, shallow thrusts.

Good points: Again, quite a dominant position for the guy, allowing him to push down on her with each thrust. He can easily fondle her breasts and — by opening her knees — lean forward to kiss her. Because of the angle of penetration here, the shaft of your cock should also be able to brush against her clitoris.

Bad points: Not a great deal of scope for moving around. She may object to being folded up like a parcel. And she won't be able to do much with her hands, either.

Lean forwards to tease her nipples during sex.[3]

Keep her steady by squeezing your thighs around her butt.

[3] *Especially if they have ginger hair and wear glasses.*

84

POSITION 13 *The Hand Grip*

How to do it: You kneel forwards and point your erection downwards so that it meets her vagina, supporting yourself by gripping her hands. Be careful not to put too much weight on her, however.

Good points: With her thighs wide open and her legs stretched out behind you, this is an extremely horny, pornographic position. Although penetration isn't particularly deep, it allows you to lean forwards to kiss her mouth, neck and breasts.

Bad points: Very tiring, especially for her. And you can't use your hands.

Raise her arse to the required level by using a cushion or pillow.

Interlock your fingers or you'll fall over once the going gets good.

85

POSITION 14 *The Collar*

RATINGS

How to do it: She lies on her back with her hips raised to facilitate entry, and places her feet on your shoulders. You support her weight with your thighs.

Good points: If she keeps her thighs together as much as possible, this position will 'tighten' her vagina. It also provides an excellent angle for deep penetration, and both of you may find the submissive nature of it very arousing. Plus, she can easily reach between her legs to masturbate while you fuck her.

Bad points: You have to do most of the thrusting, although she can help by gripping your legs or forearms.

At orgasm, she can pull you forwards by crossing her ankles.

The closer you keep your body to her legs, the deeper the penetration will be.

POSITION 15 *The Open Wide*

How to do it: She lies on her back with her legs pulled up, and you hold them in place with your arms.

Good points: This is one of the best positions for deep penetration, so make sure she's fully turned on before attempting it. It's also one of the most dominant, so you're totally in charge of how hard and how fast you wish to thrust.

Bad points: If you have a big cock, you have to be careful or you could cause your lover pain with this one. It's also tiring on the arms, which have to bear all your weight.

Keep her thighs tucked out of the way to ensure maximum penetration.

POSITION 16 *The Lazy Kneel*

RATINGS

How to do it: She lies back on the bed with her legs over the side, and you kneel in front of her on the floor. Depending on the height of your bed, you may need to use cushions to get the angle right.

Good points: No weight on your arms, so it won't be tiring even if you're not exactly Brian '*Superstars*' Jacks. Very easy to touch her breasts and clitoris while you're at it.

Bad points: You'll be quite far apart from each other, so kissing is out of the question.

She can easily reach down to masturbate herself.

Hold onto her hips to stop her sliding away from you on the 'outstroke'.

POSITION 17 *The Riding High*

How to do it: You squat astride her, arching your back so your cock is at the right angle to enter her pussy. She can support you by folding her legs behind your arse.

Good points: Excellent for clitoral stimulation because you're coming 'down' on her. As you're holding her thighs together with yours, her pussy will seem tighter than usual.

Bad points: Shallow penetration, so small-cocked guys can expect to slip out quite a lot. Plus, you have to be cautious when thrusting or you might bruise your penis.

Use short thrusts to ensure stability.

You may need to use your hands for balance, so playing with her breasts could be a precarious business.

GIRL ON TOP *positions*

The keen-eyed amongst you[4] will have noticed that the positions in the previous section required men to do most of the 'work'. So what better to try next than some techniques in which you lie flat on your back, attempting nothing more athletic than a sickly leer of satisfaction?

Not that your partner will think you're lazy if you guide her into a 'girl on top' (or 'cowgirl') position. On the contrary, she'll probably be delighted, because it'll give her a chance to set the pace and rhythm of sex, to regulate the depth to which your cock penetrates her, and to generally be the dominant one in bed. As well as all this, these positions afford her much more room for manoeuvre than when you're squashing her, so she'll find it easier to reach down and touch her clitoris during sex.

Visually, too, they are a treat. You can usually see your penis sliding in and out of her pussy, and her breasts will be displaying their natural heft instead of disappearing towards her armpits. On the minus side, it'll be harder for you to control your orgasm, so premature ejaculators should be ready to warn their partner when matters are approaching meltdown. You should also make sure that you're good and hard before initiating this kind of shag — a floppy cock is more likely to slip out, and if she brings her weight down on it you could be looking at the sort of groin/pain interface more commonly associated with peasant being asked to sign a confession by the Chilean Rapid Response Police Squad.

One last point before we get onto the dirty pictures. It will really improve your pleasure if your girlfriend is fit enough to squat up on the soles of her feet, rather than simply rest her shins on either side of you. In this position, she can add all manner of delightful twists and figure-of-eight swivels to the proceedings as she rises and falls. So, just as she may be using her subtle feminine wiles to encourage you to lose weight from your gut,[5] you could do worse than tell her to use the step machine next time she's at the gym.

---

[4] *Owls, for instance.*

[5] *Usually with the phrase 'You disgust me, you tub of lard'.*

POSITION 18 *The Jockey*

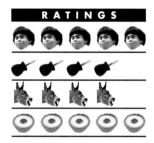

RATINGS

How to do it: You lie down as though out sparko, and she sits on her haunches (and your penis). She may need to put her hands on your chest for balance, and you can use yours to stroke her thighs or breasts.

Good points: If she opens her legs, you'll be treated to some very horny views of her riding your cock. This is an ideal position for her to show off her virtuosity in the saddle. Also, it offers excellent penetration.

Bad points: Tiring for her. You can't really do much thrusting, so you may feel a mite submissive.

You can reach up to cup and play with her breasts.

Keep your legs stretched out flat so you don't dislodge her.

POSITION 19 *The Lazy Jockey*

RATINGS

How to do it: As the name suggests, this is a less vigorous version of the previous style, mainly because she can rest on her lower legs and sit back on your thighs.

Good points: It's easier to fondle her tits like this, and — providing you're not a complete slob — you can easily sit up and kiss them too. She has both hands free to pleasure you (or herself) with.

Bad points: Penetration, though still impressive, isn't quite so deep as in 'The Jockey', and she'll find it harder to do any gymnastic trickery.

Put your thumb against her clitoris to provide stimulation as she rides you.

You can help set the rhythm by gripping her waist.

POSITION 20 *Backwards Cowgirl*

RATINGS

How to do it: You lie on your back with your knees apart and slightly raised. She sits between them facing the other way.

Good points: All the advantages of doggy style, but without the carpet burns, this allows you to massage her back and buttocks while you fuck. You can easily finger her anus, and she can reach down to fondle your balls. Best of all, she can lean forwards until she finds the perfect angle for G-spot stimulation.

Bad points: Can feel a bit impersonal if you get your jollies from eye contact. And it's a law that you have to keep saying how nice and small her arse looks.

Reach up to caress her spine or pull on her hair.

The faceless aspect of this position makes it ideal if you want to fantasise about making love to someone else.

93

POSITION 21 *The Nice Lie Down*

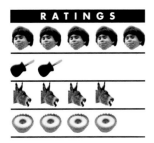

RATINGS

How to do it: Yup, you're flat on your back again, but this time you have to take her weight because she stretches out on top of you, getting as much skin to skin contact as possible.

Good points: She can rotate her hips to give very different sensations to the usual in-out-in-out ones. If she's a tall girl, you can kiss deeply while you fuck.

Bad points: Because she doesn't support herself on her elbows, she could squash the breath out of you if she's been packing away the cakes recently. And the slowness of this style makes it a bit 'Sunday morning' for more athletic tastes.

Her movements should be slow
and subtle, rotating and grinding
rather than rising and falling.

She can rest her feet
on yours to give
added purchase.

POSITION 22 *Criss-Cross*

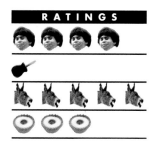

RATINGS

How to do it: Sit up with your legs outstretched while she sits facing you. Lean back and grip each other by the ankles. Let her do the rocking back and forth.

Good points: It's different, and it has a nice element of mutual bondage as you're holding each other in place. Superb views of her pussy writhing on your cock.

Bad points: A bit unwieldy, and penetration is quite shallow. Also it bloody hurts your ankles if she puts too much weight on them.

Kissing is impossible, so make the best use of eye contact to turn each other on.

Don't try to tug on her legs to help the rhythm — it won't work.

POSITION 23 *The Interlocking Position*

RATINGS

How to do it: She wraps her legs over your arms while sitting between your legs. You hold her in position by resting your hands on her back.

Good points: She can lean forwards to kiss you. You can toy with her nipples. And you feel a bit of a stud, frankly, for even knowing this position exists outside of a game of 'Twister'.

Bad points: No picnic to get into, and once you're there penetration is nothing to write home about. Movement is also fairly restricted.

You need to be gentle in your exertions, as there's a good chance of your dick falling out if you attempt anything too hammer-and-tongs.

If she rests back on her hands, it frees yours up to caress her.

POSITION 24 *Rising to the Trot*

How to do it: You sit upright and she goes astride you, crossing her legs and holding onto your back for support.

Good points: She can only really generate any bouncing motion by squeezing her thighs up and down, so for many women this position is reminiscent of horse-riding. As this action will cause her vaginal muscles to contract, you should feel subtle waves of pleasure as though your penis was being 'milked'. It's also a great one for touching and kissing her tits.

Bad points: The gentle rocking motion may be a little tame for some tastes. And if you're a fat bloke, she won't be able to get close to your cock.

Ideal for kissing her neck and breasts.

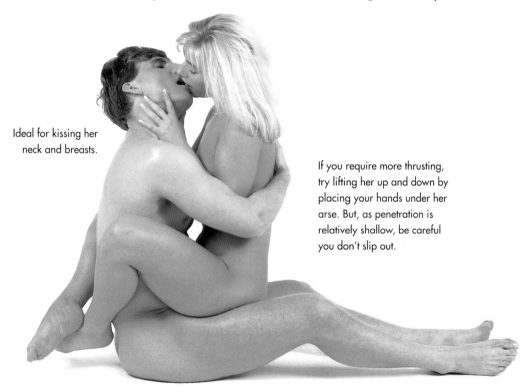

If you require more thrusting, try lifting her up and down by placing your hands under her arse. But, as penetration is relatively shallow, be careful you don't slip out.

POSITION 25 *The Crucifix*

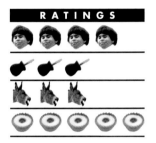

RATINGS

How to do it: Once again, you're out flat on your back like one of the boy Tyson's opponents, except this time you have your arms outstretched. She climbs aboard, linking hands with you, and you mutually flex your arm muscles to help her rise and fall.

Good points: Excellent for kissing while your fuck, and if she's quite light you can get a surprising amount of movement going. You may also get turned on by the faux bondage element here.

Bad points: Definitely a bit too subtle for some tastes, and she'll need to have good control of her vaginal muscles or you're not really going to get anywhere. Also, if she's a bit of a porker, you could end up going blue in a hurry.

Lots of arousing
skin-to-skin contact.

She can press her
feet against yours
to help movement.

POSITION 26 *Crossed Legs*

RATINGS

How to do it: She sits in a loose lotus position on top of you, resting one hand (and as much of her weight as possible) back on your knees. You support her by holding her up with your thighs and hands.

Good points: If you're knackered, then this allows her to masturbate and to be totally in charge of things. She can rub your erection over her vaginal lips and clitoris in between strokes, and she can angle it so that her G-spot is stimulated. All you have to do is watch.

Bad points: Her crossed legs mean you can't actually see that much action. And if she's lardy, you could end up feeling that you've been run over by a bus.

You can lick your fingers and reach up to her nipples while she bobs away.

If your cock is long and flexible enough, she can lean back to get different sensations in her pussy.

POSITION 27 *The Seesaw*

How to do it: You sit up with your legs extended and quite wide apart, holding her with your hands so she can lean backwards. She grips your arms and lowers herself onto your cock.

Good points: Easy to lavish attention on her breasts with your mouth.

Bad points: It's pretty hard to thrust in this position, and you can only use one hand on her tits or she'll be in danger of falling backwards. The angle of penetration isn't particularly comfortable if you've got major wood.

Use one hand to caress her neck, spine and hair.

POSITION 28 *Lying Back*

How to do it: You're sitting with your legs open wide enough for her to lie in between them. Once you've pulled her onto your erection (which will have to be held down to facilitate entry), you can hold her knees together to 'tighten' her vagina. She rests up on her elbows.

Good points: You're very close to the action if you pop your cork by watching her pussy doing the old sword swallowing act. Unlike most other 'girl on top' positions, you can dictate the pace by pulling her thighs back and forth. Also, the angle of your cock is certain to stimulate her G-spot.

Bad points: You really have to bend your cock down to get it in. She can't use her hands to any productive purpose.

You can reach down to touch her clitoris.

Don't try any extravagant thrusts, or your cock will flip out.

POSITION 29 *The Wraparound*

RATINGS

How to do it: This is pretty much a human knot, so I wouldn't recommend it on a first date. What you do is sit with your legs crossed and get her to lower herself onto you, bracing herself on your thighs and curling her legs around your ribs.

Good points: Both of you can set the rhythm by lifting and pushing against each other. You're close enough in to be able to bite or kiss each other's necks, lips and shoulders.

Bad points: Frankly, a bit uncomfortable for both parties, so don't even think about it if you've got backache. Plus, she can't touch your balls and you can't reach her pussy, so it's only worth a crack if she gets off on vaginal sex.

Tug gently back on her hair so you can kiss the length of her neck.

She can push off your knees to get 'lift'.

POSITION 30 *Leaning Back*

RATINGS

How to do it: She wraps her legs around your back, leaning her weight back and supporting herself by grasping your ankles. Your hands are free to caress her back, armpits or breasts.

Good points: If she's light enough to be manhandled, you can jog her up and down on your erection. You have both hands free to explore her body. It's easy to lean forwards and kiss.

Bad points: Neither of you can touch her clitoris, and this position won't work too well if you've got a beer gut.

Ask her to move her hands every now and then, or your shins will start to ache.

If her legs are short, she won't be able to cross them behind you.

103

REAR ENTRY *positions*

It is a matter of no small mystery to me how something as pleasurable as rear entry sex ever got the nickname 'doggy style'. Because anyone who has ever watched dogs fuck will be able to tell you that they have absolutely *no* style at all. I mean, we're talking about an animal whose idea of foreplay consists of drooling, and which will gladly hump furniture or your trouser leg if it can't find a slow enough bitch to rape in the local park.

Similarly, when people talk about rear-entry sex being good because 'it brings out an animal instinct', I begin to wonder if they've ever seen any of those nature programmes on TV. Because, whether David Attenborough happens to be pointing his camera at bugs, baboons or birds, one thing is immediately clear — they sure don't look as though they're enjoying it much. The females, especially, can forget any human refinements like cunnilingus or the multiple orgasm: a good fuck for them is one where they don't actually fall out of the tree afterwards. In short, whoever it was who wrote that 'Nature is red in tooth and claw' might just as easily have added 'and it sure as hell doesn't own too many Barry White records either.'

With regards to the human race,[6] however, rear-entry sex is one of the very finest ways available for achieving mutual ecstasy. Penetration is nearly always extremely deep, the penis is angled to chafe agreeably on the G-spot, and — because there's no eye contact — both partners have free rein to fantasise about making love to a mystery partner. As well as this, her breasts will be more sensitive because gravity will increase the bloodflow to the nipples, and your scrotum will brush against the soft cushion of her buttocks with each stroke. OK, on the down side, it's easy for anyone with a hairtrigger to lose it in this position, precisely because it's such a visual and sensual feast, but — hey! — look on the bright side. What other position allows you both to pull utterly abandoned 'come faces' without worrying that you look like a Romanesque gargoyle?

---

[6] *Which, spookily enough, was the exact same message found on a charred greetings card near Roswell, New Mexico, in 1947.*

POSITION 31 *The... oh, alright then... Doggy Style*

RATINGS

How to do it: She gets down on all fours as though searching for a lost contact lens, and you plug yourself in from behind. Easy.

Good points: She's going to feel plenty of even the smallest cock in this position. During sex, she can reach back and touch her clitoris or your balls, and you can lean over to cup her breasts. Plus, if you get the timing right, you can both do the thrusting.

Bad points: Both your knees may suffer from carpet burn, and short-legged fellows may need to prop themselves up with cushions or switch to the Rifleman (see position 33).

If you're fat, you can rest your belly on 'nature's shelf' — her arse.

By sliding a finger down the crevice of her butt cheeks, you can stimulate her anus while you screw.

105

POSITION 32 *Passive Rear Entry*

RATINGS

How to do it: It's essential that you use a soft bed for this one, as the floor — even if lushly carpeted — will be too hard for her. Once you're on top of the duvet, she lies down with her legs parted enough for you to fit in between them. Ride away in the press-ups pose, taking care not to collapse on top of her.

Good points: Very submissive for her. Presuming she likes that sort of thing.

Bad points: Penetration is pretty shallow for a rear-entry position, the view is terrible, and neither of you can do anything useful with your hands.

Arch your lower back to get extra penetration.

POSITION 33 *The Rifleman*

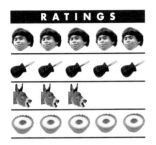
How to do it: As with Doggy Style, she's on all fours and you're stationed behind her. However, you go up on one knee, which will raise the height of your tackle about 3 inches. This could be crucial if you're a bit shorter than her.

Good points: All the advantages of doggy, but with the added bonus that it stops you clambering all over her like a climbing frame.

Bad points: None whatsoever.

Don't try to go up on both your haunches — you'll look like a goblin taking a dump.

POSITION 34 *Riding Backwards*

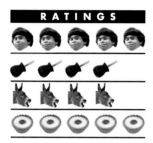

RATINGS

How to do it: You lean back on your arms, she squats on you and leans forwards on hers.

Good points: She does all the humping, and can angle your penis inside her for maximum satisfaction. If your legs are open wide enough, she can reach back to caress your balls.

Bad points: You're a bit inactive, and it can be a strain on the back and arms. She's laughing, mind you.

Once she has come, she can up the ante for you by squatting on her soles intead of her shins. This will provide a real show and guarantee deeper thrusts.

POSITION 35 *Standing Doggy*

RATINGS

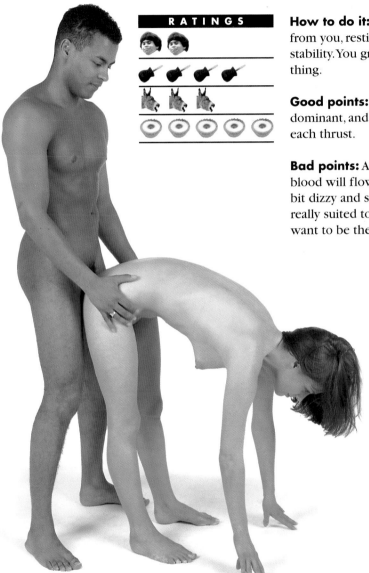

How to do it: She bows down facing away from you, resting her palms on the floor to add stability. You grip her waist and do your bad thing.

Good points: Top notch penetration, extremely dominant, and you can control the depth of each thrust.

Bad points: As her head is pointing down, blood will flow there, possibly making her feel a bit dizzy and short of breath. So this one is only really suited to a quickie fuck in which you want to be the boss.

Try not to tug her back and forth too much, as it's hard enough for her to maintain balance already.

She should spread her arms as wide as possible to maintain stability.

POSITION 36 *Reverse Cowgirl*

RATINGS

How to do it: You lean back and she sits slightly sideways on top of you, with one leg passing over yours, and one underneath. She provides all the motion necessary by rising and falling on her thighs.

Good points: You can kiss her neck, and she can use her two free hands to rub her clitoris and your balls simultaneously.

Bad points: You're pretty much the passenger in this one, so it would be a bit of a damp squib if you feel particularly randy and active.

If her hair is long, she should be careful not to toss it back into your face too often.

She can touch herself while she rides you.

SIDE-BY-SIDE *positions*

Very much the poor relation of the three main sexual styles, side-by-side positions (and I'm including here, for the sake of argument,[7] standing-up sex) are nevertheless worth trying, especially if your erotic life is getting jaded. They offer plenty of body contact and hands-free action, there's no danger of being crushed by a fat partner, and they are ideal for comfort if your lover is up the duff. Best of all, standing-up sex is superb for dangerous or outdoor quickies, whether they're up against a tree, in a shop changing room, or 35,000 feet high in the luxurious surrounds of an aircraft khazi.

The only real problems crop up if you and your partner are noticeably different in height, in which case the knee-bending and back-arching necessary to hit the bullseye make them more trouble than they're worth.

It's also relevant here that one of the most popular and intimate sexual positions falls into the 'side by side' category. Known to most people as 'spoons' — but, bizarrely, to men in the Armed Forces as 'a lazy sailor' — it's almost unique amongst sexual positions because neither partner has to do any work. And, just as Marilyn Monroe once remarked that 'ageing, powerful men seem to prefer me on my hands and knees', so it might be pointed out that 'knackered couples who feel horny but don't want to miss out on watching *Friends* while having sex prefer doing it on the sofa like spoons. I mean, so they can watch the TV at the same time.'

Although, admittedly, that's less catchy.

---

[7] And it's worth noting, if you do want an argument, that I am a personal friend of 'dodgy' Dave Courtney. And he's got a gun.

POSITION 37 *Sideways On*

RATINGS

How to do it: Piece of cake — you lie full length next to each other, she raises her top leg so you can slip your old fella in, then you put your leg on top of hers to 'close the door' again.

Good points: Once you are holding her top leg down with yours, her pussy will be tight as a drum, guaranteeing great friction for you and — given the proximity of your groins — lots of stimulation for her as well. You can also do a lot of cuddling and hugging in this position, which the ladies love, eh?

Bad points: Penetration isn't amazing, and the whole event may be a little too gentle for some tastes.

Her entire genital area will be pressed against yours, ensuring plenty of sensation.

The higher up you go, the more the shaft of your cock will rub against her clitoris.

POSITION 38 *Stand Up*

How to do it: Supporting one of her legs with your arm, you bend at the knee until you're able to get your cock inside her. Brace the leg she is wrapped around so she can use it to help her thrust back at you. It's also a good idea to do this up against a wall rather than free-standing.

Good points: Lots of kissing and stroking of arse, breasts and back. And having a quickie is always fun and liberated because she's probably not expecting to get an orgasm out of it.

Bad points: A bit unwieldy. And a disaster if she's taller than you. I mean, you'd need a trampoline to get anywhere.

She can grasp your shoulders or neck for balance.

Most of the thrusting will come solely from your hips, so make like early Elvis.

113

POSITION 39 *The Scissors*

How to do it: So called because it looks in profile like a pair of scissors,[8] this position is really only viable for the guy who's packing a large cock. She guides you inside her then places both her legs over yours.

Good points: You get to feel her arse a lot. And, of course, her breasts and lips are ready and waiting.

Bad points: Anything under 6 inches just isn't going to be in far enough to light the blue touchpaper, I'm afraid.

[8] *And also because I'm running out of dumb names for sexual positions.*

Pull her down onto your cock with each thrust or you may slip out.

POSITION 40 *Spoons*

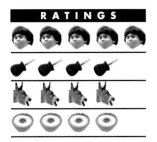

RATINGS

How to do it: Ideal for making love on a sofa if you're both watching TV, this is one of the simplest and least strenuous positions to pull off. Just lie behind her on your side, raise her top leg until you can slide your cock home, then gently thrust in and out.

Good points: You're entirely skin-to-skin, and you can hug or caress every part of her. Kissing the sensitive nape of her neck couldn't be easier.

Bad points: You won't be able to French kiss without one of you ending up in a neck brace. She can't really do much to you with her hands.

Reach round to touch her clitoris or breasts while you fuck.

Hold onto her hip to keep things stable.

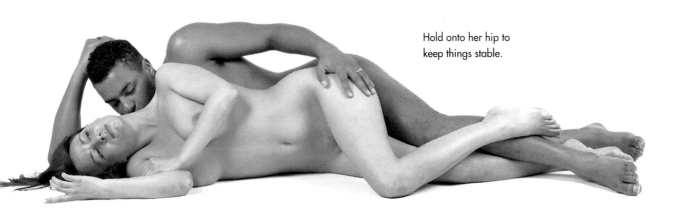

115

POSITION 41 *The Grab*

How to do it: You lean back against the wall, and your girlfriend grips her hands around your neck. You then help to pull her up, holding onto her thighs or arse for support. She gets what foothold she can on the wall behind you, and the fun begins. Alternatively, you can swap over so she's against the wall.

Good points: Ideal for a quickie in a cupboard or a train khazi, and it could give you a kick just to know that you're strong enough — and your girlfriend is slim enough — to manage this.

Bad points: For anyone who hasn't been pumping iron, this is a real trial. And, given that you can't really get a lot of movement, it's frankly a long ride for a short slide. On a more practical note, there's also a chance that your wall will for ever bear the marks of your girlfriend's dirty toes. So best save this one for when you're staying in a hotel, eh?

Get your hands as far under her as possible, or your neck is going to really hurt the next morning.

Brace yourself firmly against the wall to ensure you can get some thrust.

POSITION 42 *The Entwined Position*

RATINGS

How to do it: You lie parallel to each other, with your lower legs stretched out straight. Your top legs cross over, with hers wrapping around your butt.

Good points: Great for kissing and stroking each other's bodies, and she can set the tempo by pulling you in with her foot. Penetration is actually pretty good for a side-by-side style, but as her pussy is 'open', it won't feel so tight around a little fella.

Bad points: This is a very 'loving' position, as opposed to one suited to primeval and abandoned banging, so there isn't much action. Also, while you can use your fingers to stimulate her arse, she has no chance of returning the favour.

As you're so close together, there's no chance of clitoral stimulation. So stick to caressing her arse.

Wrap your foot around her calf to get extra grip.

117

POSITION 43 *Standing Behind*

RATINGS

How to do it: She braces herself against the wall, with her feet apart. You bend down to enter her, then stand up, lifting her off the ground if necessary.

Good points: At last, a position that's superb for small guys, as the less you have to lift her, the easier it's going to be. That said, it's not really as comfortable as standard doggy, and its main attraction seems to be that you can kiss her neck while screwing.

Bad points: Another one that's going to do your magnolia walls no favours, I'm afraid. And it's very submissive for the woman, so don't expect her to do anything fancy with her hands. Unless she's double-jointed.

The wider apart her feet are, the easier it will be for you to gain entry.

COMPLEX *positions*

Although they failed to come up with the concept of 'the sandwich' until well into the eighteenth century, our ancestors nevertheless proved themselves to be highly inventive creatures. Nowhere is this ingenuity of mind so clearly demonstrated than in the number of ways they devised to make love. In fact, you might be surprised to learn that — from the Romans to the Mayans to the Samurai — they conceived of over 500 different sexual positions.

However, I've picked just seven 'complex' ones for this book, because I honestly believe that no one likes having to constantly rearrange their body parts during sex.[9] And frankly, even these seven should be saved until your love life gets really, really boring and you've tried all the other normal stuff, because they are neither comfortable nor easy to carry off. In short, try these on a first date and your new lover is probably going to think you just got out of jail. After serving a very long sentence for a very weird crime.

That's not to say there aren't any good things about them, of course. For starters, they are probably a lot 'dirtier' than most of the stuff you and your partner have done before, and — whatever your parents, your teachers and your priest may have told you — sometimes it's nice to be filthy. Also, to be a truly open and adventurous lover, you can't afford to turn your nose up at new ideas, however strange they may seem. Your motto has to be 'try anything once'.

So, if you're in good shape, it's a special occasion, and your girlfriend gives you the green light, you could do worse than check these out and get weaving.

---

[9] *With the obvious exception of Mr Potato Head.*

119

POSITION 44 *The Turn*

RATINGS

How to do it: You lie back while she rides you, cowgirl style. Then, using her hands to steady herself, she lifts one leg over your body and begins to turn sideways. She carries on rotating, stopping at each point of the compass for a few thrusts until she's gone full circle.

Good points: You get a unique corkscrew feeling on your cock while she turns around, and — like one of those 'multiple' postcards from a holiday resort — you get a full view of all the goodies she's got.

Bad points: She needs to be very nimble and very wet to manage this. And it's best to hold onto her in case she slips, doing you a very nasty injury in the process.

Keep still and let her do the majority of thrusting, or else it'll feel like a rodeo for her.

Tell her to take
each turn slowly.
It'll be safer.

As each new
angle of her
body swings into
view, make sure
to caress and
compliment it.

121

POSITION 45 *The Slide*

RATINGS

How to do it: Jesus, this isn't easy, but if you're determined to have a crack, then kneel down and lift your girlfriend's legs up to your shoulders. Next, holding your erection downwards, slide it into her. Anyone packing less than seven inches need not apply.

Good points: Well, it's probably more fun than cribbage. But only just.

Bad points: For you? Well, bending your cock like this won't be terrifically comfy, but you've still got by far the easier draw here. As well as strain on her lower back and creases in her stomach, she's soon going to find the blood rushing to her head. In short, for show-offs only.

Make sure she doesn't try to cross her feet behind your neck. Although it will give her support, it'll put you in traction.

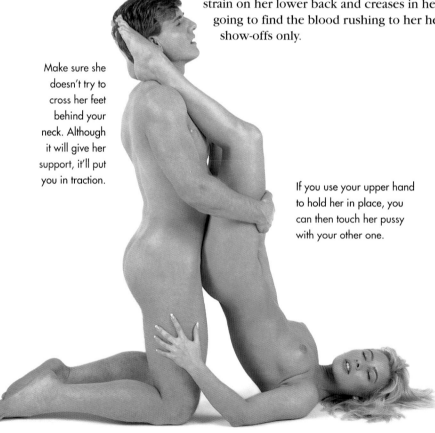

If you use your upper hand to hold her in place, you can then touch her pussy with your other one.

POSITION 46 *The Wishbone*

How to do it: Slightly more tricky to arrange than 'a quiet night in' with Oliver Reed, this is one sexual position that you'll actually have to choreograph beforehand. She starts by lying across the bed, with one leg raised, then you slide in behind her at right angles. Next, bend your legs forwards so she can hold your ankles, then grip onto her shoulders to provide purchase for your thrusts.

Good points: Another one for your collection of novelties. Plus, she can give your feet a good rub down…

Bad points: Apart from the palaver involved in getting into this shape, you'll probably find that it makes her lower leg go numb after a few minutes.

If you grip with your lower hand, you can reach around to stroke her breasts.

The wider she can open her legs, the deeper you'll penetrate.

POSITION 47 *The Missionary Turn*

How to do it: Similar to 'The Turn' except that *you* have to be the one fit enough to appear on *Gladiators*. The trick is to keep as much weight off her as possible, and to slowly swivel your body around in a circle without letting your cock slip out.

Good points: Gives you a chance to explore every part of her body, from head to toes. The different angles of penetration will also afford both of you a full range of sensations.

Bad points: Bloody exhausting on the arms, and at one point you need to bend your cock backwards — no picnic if you've got major wood. Plus, it's pretty essential that she keeps quite still during the proceedings, and at one stage she also has to look right at your arse crack. And, well, it's not Venice, is it?

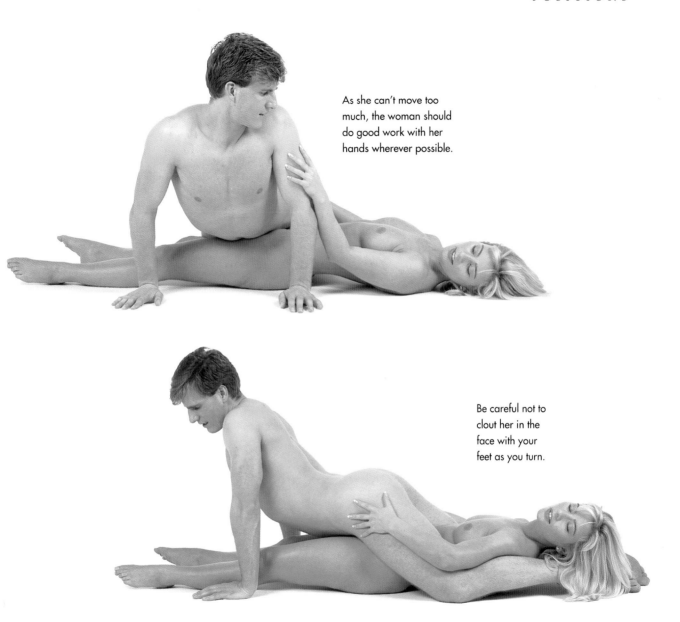

As she can't move too much, the woman should do good work with her hands wherever possible.

Be careful not to clout her in the face with your feet as you turn.

POSITION 48 *The Toilet Seat*

RATINGS

How to do it: Romantically named it may not be, but this one is worth trying if you want to give her a new sensation. You lie on your back with your knees drawn up, as though preparing to do that odd 'bicycling in the air' routine gym teachers used to be so keen on. She squats down on your penis and lifts herself up and down to provide the action.

Good points: If her breasts are nice, then they will jiggle about appealingly in any handily-placed mirrors as she bobs away. And if you have 'submission' fantasies, then this will really put gravy on your goose.

Bad points: Your cock feels a bit squashed between your thighs, and once again it has to be bent back. Touching each other is well-nigh impossible if you want to keep your balance. And you need to be fit to last more than a few seconds.

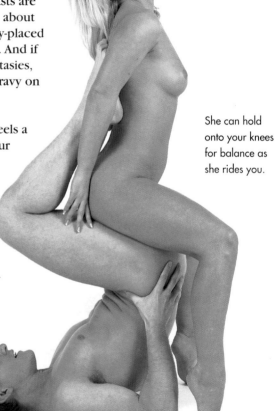

She can hold onto your knees for balance as she rides you.

If you get tired, she can turn 180°, allowing you to lean both your backs against a wall.

POSITION 49 *The Fold Up*

RATINGS

How to do it: You make like a four-legged creature, and she lies underneath, pulling back on her ankles until her pussy is raised up to meet your groin. A cushion or two under her lower back will help matters immensely.

Good points: Fantastically deep penetration, ensuring that even the cruelly ill-equipped will feel like they could audition for *Boogie Nights*. Also, it's reassuringly filthy.

Bad points: You can't caress her, and she's so busy holding her legs in place that she won't be able to do much either. She'll need to have signed up for a few stretching exercises too.

It's up to you to do the thrusting as she is (almost literally) tied up.

Be careful not to trap her hair under your hands — it'll hurt.

POSITION 50 *The Wheelbarrow*

RATINGS

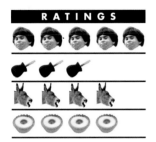

How to do it: Stand behind her, then lift her up by her thighs, pulling her back onto your cock while she supports herself on her hands. It's actually possible to walk around the room while doing this one, but she might appreciate it more if you just stick to thrusting.

Good points: So long as she's not too heavy, you can get some good in-out motion going here. And if laughing is as much a part of your love life as it should be, then you're sure to get some fun out of this.

Bad points: Neither of you can use your hands for anything exciting, and she may get a rush of blood to the bonce.

If she's really light, you can support her with just one arm held under her stomach.

CHAPTER FIVE
out of the
bedroom

Although there are some activities which are undeniably suited to just one place,[1] sex is not one of them. In fact, if you restrict your love life to the bedroom, you'll be missing out on lots of fun and probably speeding up your relationship's inevitable descent into drudgery and routine. As well as the great outdoors (which, along with cinemas, cars and restaurants will be covered later in this chapter), the other rooms of your house contain a surprisingly broad array of props and possibilities to spice things up. If you share a flat, the fear of discovery will also add a welcome jolt of adrenalin to proceedings, although you should bear in mind that people rarely look elegant when caught in the act of sex — as I can personally attest, having once walked in on a fellow student who was masturbating with the aid of a half-full jar of Bovril.[2]

Nevertheless, you are a guy, and it's a medical fact that guys can't resist a challenge. Nowhere is this more true than in the arena of sex, where males feel a strong imperative not only to make a pass at every woman they meet, but also to christen every room, bus shelter and park bench in their immediate post code, a bit like a dog marking its territory. If you find this hard to believe, then I refer you to this news item, which appeared in *The Times* of 3 August 1994:

'A couple were making love in a tree top in Windsor Great Park yesterday when the woman fell from the branches and broke her leg. A park spokesman said: "They had apparently gone to the Great Park for a bit of nookie and decided to climb the oak tree to add a bit of excitement to the session. The woman slipped from one of the branches, and had to lie there, in pain and stark naked, while her boyfriend hastily pulled on some clothes and ran to a phone box to call for help. The ambulance crew couldn't believe their eyes."'

Although it's easy to laugh, you should realise that the guy in question was merely following the same instinct for adventure which led other, admittedly more happily married, men to land on the moon, discover America and climb Everest. In fact, we should salute his spirit, however extreme the results, because he's proving a point for all of us: if the choice of venue for coition was left to women, we'd only ever make love in crisp white bedlinen. And we'd probably have to plump the pillows up afterwards as well.

Instead, using Guy Sex Opportunity Vision, your home can be seen as an adventure playground of possibilities. There is no sofa, armchair, table, work surface or flooring which cannot be adapted for intercourse.[3] I myself

---

[1] eg., waving white flags and Italy.

[2] Slogan: 'Mmm, it's beefy.'

[3] Note to Arts Council Grant Awarding Committees: it's worth mentioning that a lesser writer might have attempted a joke about pouffes here.

have even attempted to get laid on a sturdy set of freestanding bookshelves in the past, only giving in when my lover's carefully alphabetised paperbacks began to topple into an unruly pile on the floor. OK, it didn't work, but at least we tried, and you too should see your home as similar to the Cluedo board, with

WARNING! WARNING! WARNING!
Very unwieldy, and possibly
psychologically-disturbing metaphor
approaching...

your chick cast as Dr Black, getting murdered by your candlestick of love in every possible chamber and manner available, occasionally involving her 'secret passage'.

On the practical side, you might need to temper your libido long enough to make sure the surfaces you intend to use are safe and clean. Sofas are clearly very suitable for sex, but you should remove any teetering ashtrays and vacuum out any deep deposits of food particles, loose change and 'crack fluff' if you expect your sweet-smelling girlfriend to share your enthusiasm. If you're intending to pull your penis out at orgasm, you'll also need to have tissues handy, or — at worst — make sure your sofa is covered in the sort of old-fashioned chintz that IKEA gets so het up about these days. Handsome though the primary colours of Swedish furniture are, it's undeniable that a traditional pattern of flowers, leaves and small

woodland animals makes a much better disguise for a semen stain. Or, even better, buy an easy-to-wipe couch at a place like Kingdom of Leather.[4]

If you are really bold, you might get a buzz from making out in *other people's* houses. This is easy enough to do at a party ('We're just going upstairs. To put our coats in the spare bedroom. Shouldn't take more than, oh, ten minutes...'), but for a proper thrill, try the famous 'Estate Agent shag'. This is where you check out the properties for sale in the window of your local branch of Thieving, Pondlife & Scumsucker, and ask to be shown round the most palatial as prospective buyers. Once inside, you look really keen and ask the person showing you around if you can have a few minutes alone 'to discuss things'. With pound signs flashing in his eyes, he'll be happy to take a back seat while you two snuck up to the bedroom (or wherever) and make merry.

There is, however, one caveat to bear in mind before we get onto the handy tips, and that is Avoid Glass-Topped Tables. They may look serviceable enough, but I know of a case where a man was castrated when one cracked beneath his weight while fucking. Although his testicles were successfully reattached, I bet you any money *he'll* be skipping the rest of this chapter ...

---

[4] *Marketed in Eastern Europe, of course, as the Democratic Republic of Leather.*

Indoors

Chairs

Although not as versatile as a bed, chairs still offer the ambitious lover plenty of scope for enjoyment. However, you have to choose your design carefully. Comfy armchairs may look kinder on your arse, but they offer far less room for manoeuvre than those simple straight-backed ones Van Gogh used to paint. Similarly, rocking chairs and wheeled office-type chairs might seem ideal for having sex on, but the reality is that once you start screwing, they'll be harder to stay aboard than a rodeo bull. So then, go with a standard model, make sure it's sturdy enough to support the weight of two people, lay down cushions on any metal or wicker bits, and then give these moves a crack:

● **In your lap:** You sit upright with your legs together, making sure that you raise your balls up first so they don't get squashed between your thighs. She then reverses on top of you, putting her legs on the inside of yours, and balancing on her toes. The motion is a pretty simple bounce up and down, but you'll have plenty of fun kissing her neck and reaching round to feel her breasts and clitoris. This is doggy-style sex for the *incredibly* lazy man, and it's even better if you've got a mirror.

● **Facing each other:** As with the above, except she climbs aboard facing you. You can help her thrusts by lifting her at the waist, using your mouth to kiss her breasts and neck. The only real disadvantage is that neither of you will find it a breeze to touch her clitoris.

● **Kneeling:**
Good and pervy. She kneels down over the back of the chair, adopting roughly the same position used by pilgrims at prayer. However, as it's quite easy for the chair to topple forwards when you get vigorous, it's safer to place it facing a wall or sofa. Also, ensure that she has a cushion under her for comfort, or she'll walk like a cripple for hours afterwards.

133

The Kitchen

Sadly, a clean kitchen is a prerequisite here, so if yours is the customary bachelor slit trench, complete with a drum kit of filth-encrusted pans and its own personal termite mound, you'll have to tidy up or miss out. Once the place is gleaming, however, and once you've safely stowed away any sharp knives or fragile crockery, you can have a crack at these kinky manoeuvres. . .

● **The sink:** This is where you lift her up until she's sitting on the edge of the sink and then enter her busily from the front. Although you may have to stand on tiptoe if you're short or have a smallish cock, this discomfort is more than adequately compensated for by the proximity of running water. Even if you already have a mixer tap fitted, buy one of those cheap rubber nozzles, and use it to direct hot (but not *too* hot) jets over her arse and pussy. This will stimulate her like a vibrator while you hump, and if she is artful enough she can take over and spray it on your balls too. Best of all, when you come you'll have no worries about carpet cleaner, wet patches or Kleenex — simply climax onto the handy wipe-clean surface and wash it away.

● **The washing machine:** Many bored housewives use their washing machines to help them orgasm, usually by turning it on to full juddering spin cycle and squirming around on top so their clitoris is stimulated. Use this feature to your advantage and lean your lover against the Zanussi while you screw, taking care that you don't snag yourself on any sharp corners.

● **The fridge:** The use of foodstuffs for sexual arousal is perhaps most memorably seen in the movie *9½ Weeks*, where Mickey Rourke feeds a blindfolded Kim Basinger various objects from his cold box. And while it's fun to tease your lover's lips with fruit and veg, don't feel you have to stop at her mouth. Whipped cream, bananas, olive oil and ice cream can all be probed into or licked off her body. In fact, so long as you steer clear of anything that might irritate her — like chilli peppers, salted gherkins or taking Polaroid photographs of her while she's blindfolded and wearing a Del Monte product in her private parts — this foreplay game can last for ages.

The Shower

Another staple of the liberated lover, and ideal for soapy foreplay, full sex in the shower is actually quite tricky to get right. For instance, if you attempt it by merely bending your knees so you can enter her under the spray, you'll get

nowhere. (Except possibly in plaster, because you both slipped over and cracked your elbows.) The best method is to stand *sideways on* to the spray and have her perch her feet on the edge of the bath. Thus braced, she can lean back against the tiled wall and move up and down quite freely.

If your shower is one of those little cubicle numbers, however, this won't work, so you'll have to be a bit more inventive. Lean her against the side closest to the wall and detach the shower nozzle, directing it over her breasts before holding it between her legs. As there is still some danger of slipping here, it would be a good idea to put a towel or (ideally) a rubber bath mat on the base of the shower. Oh, and make sure the soap is in its dish, of course.

The Bath

Although easy enough to do in one of those six-man whirlpool affairs (and thanks to the thick, swirling water you can even manage this in public if your girlfriend's prepared to pretend she's just sitting in your lap), this is not as good as it sounds in a normal tub. But, as the bathroom is one place where you and your girlfriend see each other naked a lot, that isn't going to stop you trying, is it? Accordingly, here's the best method I have come up with in the course of my exhaustive research for this book: once you've soaped each other thoroughly and she can see you're in a 'periscope up' situation, lie back with your head at the opposite end to the taps. Your lover then shimmies on top of you, keeping her knees directly above yours so they don't get jammed painfully against the enamel sides. You wedge your toes against the far end of the bath and she gets purchase against the taps, and you then rock slowly back and forth. Any attempt to get vigorous will backfire, so keep it slow and easy. This will also help keep splashing down to a minimum, much to the relief of your downstairs neighbours.

Other venues

Restaurants

When a man wants to get romantic with a woman, it's even money that he'll take her out for a slap-up dinner to set the mood. Not only does this remind her what a suave operator he is, but it also gives him a chance to peer down the front of her most expensive dress and to show off his exceptional knowledge of fine wines.[5] Given this heady blend of drink and sex appeal, it's no surprise that both parties often start to feel frisky. And if that does happen, why wait until you get home?

---

[5] *Specifically, that he knows the house wine is the only one he can afford.*

● **Footsie:** Only really an option when there's a long tablecloth, and best if you both slip off your shoes beforehand. Your role is pretty much limited to stroking her calves and inner thighs with an outstretched foot because, although some women swear by it, most would hurl at the mere idea of you masturbating them with your big toe. Men, however, notoriously have less scruples, so she should lift both her feet up into your lap, having warned you to unzip your flies first. Next, by turning her soles inwards, she can grip your penis and ferry your foreskin softly up and down. (The sensation is even more novel if she's wearing silk or nylon stockings.) It's easy enough for you both to sit upright while doing this, and the only real tricks are in managing to keep a straight face and making sure you come onto the tablecloth rather than over your suit.

● **The napkin wank:** This only works if you're sitting next to each other, and it's twice as easy if you're seated in an alcove or booth. She puts her hand under the table (having ensured that she's on your left if she's right-handed, and vice versa) and subtly unzips you. Next, she wraps your napkin around your bulging member and masturbates you through it. The feel of linen is not unpleasant, and this 'invisible' method means that if you *are* detected she can pretend she was only rearranging your napkin. It's worth remembering, though, that the cheaper the restaurant you get caught doing this in, the more chance there is of you being beaten up by angry waiters.

● **In the khazi:** Restaurant khazis may not be a suite at the Ritz, but they still offer the perfect venue for a quickie between courses. The basic rule of thumb is that the Ladies is 'safer' than the Gents, but if at all possible head for the Disabled trap. This will be roomier, cleaner, far less busy, and it's also fitted with several handy 'grip bars' to hold onto when the going gets tough. Once installed, keep noise down to a minimum and choose from the three positions best suited to fucking in a confined space. These are:

a) you sitting down, with her facing away from you on your lap;
b) her bending over towards the cistern, with you entering from the rear;
c) her leaning back against the sink and mirror while you hold her thighs up with your arms.

Avoid doing it against the door, because the rattling will alert people. If you do get caught, simply insist that one of you was feeling very ill and the other came in to help. They won't believe you, but so what.

The Cinema

You don't have to know the artistic difference between *The Battleship Potemkin* and *Bachelor Party*[6] to realise that your local multiplex is a great place for foreplay. You're sitting next to each other in the dark, it's natural to cover your lap with a coat, and everyone else is too busy watching the movie to bother about what you're getting up to. Nevertheless, you can help to avoid detection by taking a few precautions. Firstly, always choose seats positioned against the side wall, as far away from the aisle as possible. Secondly — and pretty obviously — make sure that there's nobody sitting behind you. Thirdly, go for a movie that's quite 'dark' — black and white re-releases are ideal, especially if they're from the horror genre. And lastly, bear in mind the conversation that I once had with an elderly Savile Row tailor who was making me a suit:

'Do you want a zip or button fly in your trousers, sir?'

'Er… I don't know. What do you reckon?'

'Well sir, I always say buttons are so much *quieter* in the cinema …'

● **The popcorn wank:** You're sitting next to each other, she continually dips her hand in the box of popcorn on your lap… nothing wrong with that. However, if you subtly open the dovetailed paper slots on the box's underside and slip your erect penis up through the resulting hole, she will be able to wank you off with her fingertips. (But not her whole hand, alas, or the scrunching noises will be too suspicious.) If this isn't devious or satisfying enough, then you could try saving a couple of cartons from the last time you went to the flicks, and use them to construct a special 'hand-job tower'. Simply cut out one side of the box for her hand to fit through, glue a square of card an inch from the top, fill this bit with popcorn, and then you have a noiseless disguise for the next time you're bored or horny at the Odeon.

● **The fast asleep:** She pretends to doze off during a long flick, you gallantly let her rest her head on your lap. Cover her with a coat for 'warmth', undo your flies, and Bob's your uncle. To return the favour, eschew cunnilingus and instead ask her to loosen the waistband of her skirt. Slip your hand inside and toy away until she's happy. You won't even miss a frame of the movie.

● **Bra removal:** Very much a sexual show-off's technique, but none the less effective for that. It requires practice and dexterity to perfect though, so make

---

[6] *Answer: Only* Bachelor Party *has a 'donkey scene' in it. Duh.*

sure you can do it quickly before giving it a public debut. Here's how it works: slide a hand up the back of your lover's T-shirt and unclip the bra fastening. Then feed the strap nearest you down her arm, getting her to bend her elbow and pull her arm up into the T-shirt so the strap stretches over her hand. Put your hand around her far shoulder and work the other strap — and thus the whole, now liberated bra — down into your hand, balling it up so no one notices that there's a stray item of lingerie on the seat next to them. Her nipples are now at your mercy.

● **Poacher's pockets:** If you want her to give you a hand job in the cinema, your best bet is to wear a coat with 'poacher's pockets'. These incorporate a slit on the inside of the pocket, allowing the hand access to your private parts even when the coat looks to be fully buttoned up. A cheaper alternative is to wear baggy skateboarder-style trousers and cut the stitches out of the left-hand pocket. She can then feed her right hand through to your cock and — so long as you remember to keep your small change and keys on the other side to stop any jangling — you're laughing.

Outdoors

Teachers are among the lowest paid workers in the country, and there is, I believe, a good reason for this: they're stupid. Well, how else can you explain the fact that they persist in thinking they can 'build moral fibre' and 'shape a child's character' by introducing him to The Great Outdoors, when it is patently clear that the opposite is true? In fact, the adolescent brain will deliberately blot out any knowledge foisted upon it in this high-handed manner, as evidenced by the highly scientific table, opposite:

Given this state of affairs, it's fortunate that our guardians never tried to force us to make love outside. If they had, we would have been turned off one of the most exciting, frisky and generally free-wheelin' things you can do with a woman. Instead, the joys of nudity in the wild were something we had to discover for ourselves, usually under the blankets with the aid of a torch and a copy of the *National Geographic*. This praiseworthy publication, which I estimate is responsible for more teenage orgasms than any other medium (with the possible exception of those interior decorating magazines which carry advertisements for power showers), contained at

Outdoorsy type situation	Teacher says	Child thinks	Result when child grows up
On a country walk, a bird is seen with a twig in its beak.	'Look class, that's a female swallow preparing her nest.'	'He said "female swallow".'	His knowledge of ornithology is limited to dividing birdlife into 'the ones that crap on my car' and 'the ones you get from Colonel Sanders'.
On a school trip to the Alps, you see a fabulous cliff-top view.	'It makes you humble.'	'It makes you want to spit over the side.'	When sending a postcard home from a foreign holiday destination, however scenic and beautiful, he will always choose the one featuring a naked, large-breasted woman.
A meeting of the Cubs	'The reef knot is one of the most useful things you'll ever learn.'	'Yeah, yeah, yeah, just give me the badge.'	He uses Sellotape.

least one story per month about African tribes. Although dull enough to read, the *Geographic* cannily employed a photographer whose other job was presumably with the Congo edition of *Playboy* magazine, because each shot of jungle life featured hundreds of bare, bobbing breasts and — in the immortal words of *Porky's* — 'enough wool to make a sweater'.

The feverish imaginings this sparked in the mind were sufficient to ensure that all of us dreamt of making love under the stars. Even the certain knowledge that al fresco sex[7] would result in tangles with thorns, puddles

---

[7] Literally, 'up against a Renaissance wall painting'.

139

and stinging insects could not damage the allure. But this keenness to try it out doesn't mean that outdoor sex is a piece of cake. It isn't. It needs planning. So, before we get onto the specific locations, let's lay down some ground rules.

Firstly, there is the problem of light. If you're going to be adopting a 'trousers off' pose in public, you won't want to be observed. Therefore, take pains to avoid locations near a lot of street lighting, and time your assignations for when there isn't a full moon out. Remember, too, that it isn't just light you have to worry about these days: there are also close circuit TV cameras in many urban areas. (Some couples have been caught out, especially, in those all-night cashpoint lobbies, unaware that their stolen moments of bliss are being taped. This can result either in prosecution, or in a lot of nudging and winking next time they go into the bank.)

Secondly, the outdoors is of course home to all manner of animal and insect life. Although most mammals will avoid a couple making love,[8] insects are not so discriminating. As well as stinging you, they will crawl into your hair or buzz around threateningly, with this problem getting worse in the summer months and in hotter climates. Covering yourself with a layer of repellent might seem like the ideal precaution, but remember that this will make bare skin taste bad, so lay off the kissing and nibbling. Alternatively, bring *two* blankets out with you — one to lie on, and one to use as a sheet.

Lastly, try to be discreet. If people think you are screwing in public, they may be inclined to play killjoy and call the police. The trick is to make it look as though you're just cuddling each other, so keep as many clothes on as possible and stick to suitable positions. (The best is 'spoons'.) The thrill of having sex outdoors will more than compensate for any loss of variety or room for manoeuvre.

And now for some more specific ideas . . .

Parks

For people who live in the countryside, making love outdoors is easy. But in town it's a bit tougher. Most urban parks are filled with a shadowy nighttime population of junkies, tramps, muggers and 'care in the community' numbskulls, and the grass is littered with empty cider bottles and dog mess. So remember to keep your eyes peeled at all times for unwanted company, and to

---

[8] *Except for badgers, who like to grunt and play with themselves while they watch.*

Sex outdoors: Dealing with the law

Q: What is the offence called?
'Indecent exposure in a public place' (Town Police Clauses Act 1847)

Q: What is the maximum penalty?
A 'Level 3' fine (up to £1,000) or fourteen days in jail.

Q: Where do most couples get caught?
Parks, outside pubs, near houses where there are parties going on, alleyways, raves, motorway verges and hard shoulders.

Q: What happens if you're not actually having full-on sex?
You can still get done for 'breach of the peace', usually depending on how much noise you're making.

Q: What is the likelihood of going to court?
If a member of the public has called the police to complain about your antics, there's a good chance you'll be up before the beak. But if a policeman spots you on his rounds and doesn't feel you're causing offence to anyone, then he's much more likely to let you off with a caution.

Q: What excuse have they heard most often?
'We were looking for something that I dropped on the ground.'

avoid places (such as bandstands) which already contain a flotsam of used condoms, or the odds are you won't be alone for long.

● **Under a tree:** If you are going to make love in a park or square, then try to find one which has a willow tree in it. The branches hang down, forming a circular tent around the trunk, and there's enough room underneath to stretch out and do just about anything. In fact, if the foliage is thick enough, you can even screw here undetected in broad daylight. It's not called a pussy willow for nothing.

● **On the swings:** After dusk only with this method, I'm afraid, but it does add a nice twist to normal lovemaking. Get your partner to remove her knickers and sit forward in the swing, then grasp the seat with both hands. Although you can't get any enormous pendulum swings going, it's easy to rock her a few

inches back and forth. The only disadvantage is that she can't use her arms on you because she's holding onto the ropes.

● **Against railings:** You clearly need a nice quiet part of the park for this, so avoid anything adjacent to a street or your love-making will be picked out by every passing set of car headlights. Go for the railings that butt up against people's back gardens instead. Then keep to the rules of quickie sex: hike her skirt up, unzip your trousers, and grip onto the railings for jumbo thrusting power. Amusing as it might seem to combine this with some freelance bondage, you should steer clear of tying her in place with handcuffs or bike chains — trust me, you'll never find the keys in the dark.

The sea and swimming pools.

WC Fields famously remarked that he didn't drink water because 'fish fuck in it'. Well, he obviously didn't spend much time on Club 18–30 holidays, or else he'd have known that it's not just our finned brethren who get their jollies in the briny. At the current rate of progress, the Mediterranean, for example, will soon contain more used condoms than calamari. Nevertheless, sex underwater is a lot harder than it looks to do well, so try out these tips next time you're skinny-dipping:

● **Standing up:** This is the easiest position in which to have sex in the sea, mainly because you've got less chance of swallowing a mouthful of salt water than if one of you is attempting to 'float'. You can also wade in up to your necks before dropping your Speedos, and this should help you to avoid being seen by a cheering beachful of spectators. You stand up and she straddles her legs around your sides, holding onto your neck and shoulders for support. Although the stories of men being bitten on the genitals by jelly fish while doing this are grossly exaggerated, it probably won't be a great fuck technically speaking. This is because the water will counteract her natural lubrication, making your thrusts seem rough, and she'll also get a pint or two of the Med tromboned up into her pussy.

● **Snorkel doggy:** One for the shallows. You wade in to about waist height, and she bends over, immersing her face mask and snorkel under the surface. You stand behind her and take her doggy style. Although it's feasible that this may fool people watching from a few hundred yards away, anyone closer will quickly guess that you're not Mr and Mrs Jacques Cousteau. But — hey — at least your babe gets to look at fish while being shafted, and that won't happen every day.

● **Lilo sex:** This is tricky, but at least it will stop the seawater messing with her pussy's lubrication. You lie on your back on a lilo, float out of viewing distance (so make sure you're both strong swimmers), and she clambers aboard. Her legs hang over each side to stabilise the inflatable raft, and you use your foreams to lift her up and down. Again, this isn't great sex, but it will probably spice up those postcards home.

● **On the beach:** You know how irritating it feels when you put your shoes on after walking on the beach? Well, it's even worse if your whole body, including your genitals, is peppered with grains of sand. Luckily, all you have to do to stop this happening is bring a blanket along. Simple.

● **Swimming pool:** In the shallow end you can manage most sexual positions, but foreplay is trickier. Try sitting her on the edge of the pool, with her legs dangling in the water, and you'll be able to give her cunnilingus. If you find it hard to get any purchase once you start fucking, move over to the steps and hold onto them while you take her in doggy or front-on style. One word of caution, however: there are several documented cases of men getting their tackle sucked into the filtration pumps of pools, resulting in serious injury and embarrassing local newspaper headlines.

Cars

Cars are among the most common venues for teenage sexual encounters, mainly because you don't have to sneak past your parents to get inside one. And, although rather confined and uncomfortable, they do seem to strike an erotic chord with both genders, a fact that was perhaps most poetically summed up by John Travolta in *Grease*: 'With full speed on the floor they'll be waiting at the door/ You know that ain't no shit, you'll be getting loads of tit/ In Greased Lightning.' The positions you can manage will vary from model to model, with vans being the most versatile and Minis the most useless, but here are some general pointers:

● **Recline the front seat:** This is the position used by most kerb crawlers when they pick up a prostitute, and as you'd expect from that stat it's quick and easy to get into. You tip the driving seat back and lie down, while she leans over from the passenger seat to give you head. Once you're warmed up, she sits on top of you and rides away, taking care that she doesn't ram her feet against the pedals. If you prefer to be on top, just do things vice versa.

Doggers

Lovers' Lane doesn't just attract courting couples — it is also home to a specialised breed of pervert known as 'doggers'. These chaps get their rocks off by observing people having sex in parked cars, but — thanks to repeated beatings — they usually look for recognised signals that a couple wants to be watched before moving in closer than binocular range. Common codes include flashing your interior lights or dropping a hankie out of the window. If you want them to join in as well as observe, wind down the window and they will stroke you and your lover's bodies as you fuck, masturbating themselves at the same time. Watch out the next morning, however, as that may not be Turtle Wax on your bonnet . . .

143

● **Convertible doggy:** If you're lucky enough to have a car with a retractable roof, and so long as Ian McGaskell has given the weather the all clear, this is an exciting variation. Take the top down, kneel on the seats facing forwards, and give it to her doggy style while she bends over the windscreen. Privacy, of course, is essential.

● **Back seat sex:** In the cramped space of the back seat, the easiest position is the missionary. For added leg room, open the windows so she can rest her ankles on the lip outside. At a pinch, you could try doggy style, but unless you have a tall car (say, a Range Rover) you're going to have to keep your neck bent to avoid banging your head continually on the roof.

● **Hot bonnet:** If you've parked in a private place and you've left the motor running, there's fun to be had making love *on* the car rather than inside it. Just lean her over the warm bonnet, either on her back or front, and enter her briskly. The vibrations will add a twist to proceedings, but make sure your paintwork is free from dust and pigeon stools before lying her down. More importantly, for the safety of her skin and your no claims bonus, take care if your car has a large hood ornament on it (NB: Mercedes and Rolls Royce owners in particular).

● **Highway blow job:** The riskiest — and thus most exciting — kind of car sex, this takes place while you're actually in motion. In its simpler form, she puts her head in your lap and fellates you while you drive. (It's best to do this on a motorway, or else you're going to be putting on a show at the traffic lights.) The advanced version happens when *she* is driving. While operating the pedals with her feet, she leans down and sucks you off, leaving you to control the steering wheel and bark out braking instructions. Needless to say, this is highly dangerous stuff, and you could end up killing someone.

CHAPTER SIX *fun and games*

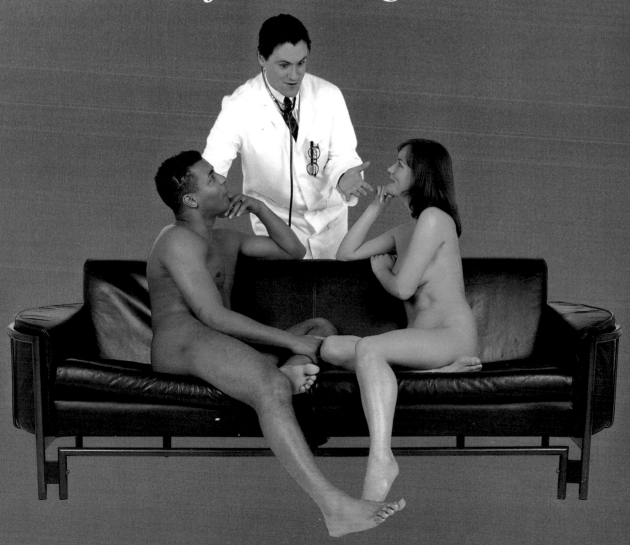

As pygmies no doubt say to each other in the showers after football, sometimes nature just isn't enough.[1] And so it may be that — through tiredness, boredom or lack of response — your lover and you require more than the usual levels of stimulation to reach orgasm. If this *is* the case, then the answer could be to bring some accessories into the bedroom.

You wouldn't be the first. There is a long history of sex toys stretching all the way back to ancient Egypt, and while the pharoahs didn't, admittedly, get much further than the clay dildo, the range of marital aids available has since expanded to fill all needs and tastes. It's a big, booming business and it attracts millions of clients (Ann Summers alone sold 400,000 vibrators in 1998), but despite this, many men still feel embarrassed about going into a sex shop. Perhaps they're worried that if they introduce sex toys to the bedroom, it will be an admission that they aren't doing the job well enough themselves. This, of course, is folly. Owning some good quality sex toys will add to your mutual enjoyment and make it easier for your lover to have orgasms, allowing you to be even more of a stud than usual. If you do feel uneasy about making a purchase, stick to mail order, or pop into an out of town shop where you're sure no-one will recognise you. Once inside, you may be surprised to find that the customers are not all dirty old men in raincoats,[2] but young, normal couples. If you're still too bashful, encourage your girlfriend to sign up for an Ann Summers party, where she can choose the toys she most likes the look of. (Call 0181 645 8320 for details of these.)

Once you've shelled out for a selection, the only real problem you face is where to keep them, as vibrators and dildos appear to be fitted with a tractor beam that locks in on people such as cleaning ladies or visiting parents. No matter how deep in that drawer full of jumpers you hide them, they will inevitably be discovered one day. My advice would be to damn the torpedoes and simply keep them in a place that's convenient for the bed. If someone discovers them, so what? To paraphrase Swift, who wrote that 'A man should never be afraid to admit he is wrong, for all he is really saying is "I am wiser now than I was yesterday"', all the revelation that you own a few arousing gadgets will say about you is that you're an open-minded lover.

With that thought firmly in mind, and with the aid of my glamorous research team and a Royal Navy battleship-size issue of K-Y Jelly, here are the ratings on some of the most popular items...

---

[1] *They also look at each other angrily and say, 'Come on! Who was picking up the guy who scored 37 headers?'*

[2] *But if you are a dirty old man who happens to be browsing through a copy of this book, get out. Everyone knows you're just waiting for a chance to take a sly look at the Rear Entry photographs.*

Plain Vibrator

Slogan: 'The Honey Pet'.
Price: £11.99 [3]
How it works: It, er, vibrates.
Good points: Comes in a discreet 'handbag' size, but still big and thick enough to be used as a dildo if she wants it like that. (Although you should note that most women use vibrators for external stimulation only.) The plain design makes it easy to clean, and — the bottom line here — it will definitely help her to climax.
Bad points: Alarmingly noisy, and it works so well that you might feel a bit of a spectator at bedtime. Also contains a baffling manufacturer's warning not to use 'on unexplained calf pain'.
Rating: 10/10. A design classic that really does the job.

Multiple-Head Vibrator

Slogan: 'Quadruple the fun!'
Price: £19.99
How it works: As above, except there are interchangeable heads, each promising to give 'unique sensations'.
Good points: Comes with a variety of different hats, each of which are easy to swap over in seconds without breaking the mood.
Bad points: Looks ridiculous, like an early prototype of the Daleks. If she has any sense of humour, she'll probably be laughing too much to climax when you whip this out.
Rating: 6/10. No real improvement on the plain vibrator.

Dildo

Slogan: 'It's your own bully boy!'
Price: £17.99
How it works: Well, Einstein, you thrust it in and out of her pussy.
Good points: Handy for bringing her off if you've lost your erection, or to penetrate her pussy if your penis is busy in another aperture. Also, with a shaft length of just under 6 inches, it's unlikely to make your cock look too shabby by comparison.
Bad points: Useless for clitoral excitement.
Rating: 5/10. It does exactly what it's meant to. But lonely women should thank God for the invention of batteries.

[3] Prices correct at the time of printing. Products available at Ann Summers and Expectations.

Giant Strap-on.

Slogan: None. And, frankly, when it's this big who needs one?
Price: £72.45 (includes leather harness)
How it works: You put it on like a belt and pretend it's yours.
Good points: You can make love to her with a massive cock for once. The sturdy leather belt holds it firmly in place throughout the most gymnastic manoeuvres, and it will never get tired. If she's a size queen, she'll be in heaven.

Bad points: You have to make her *very* wet to even get it inside, and once you're there you have to shag very slowly or she'll be 'off games' for a week. Also, your own genitals will be pressed back underneath it, so you're more likely to get a bruise than a hard on.

Rating: 8/10. You feel like the mighty Snake God. And she gets a birthday treat to remember.

Ben Wa Balls

Slogan: 'Sold as an adult novelty only.'
Price: £6.99
How they work: She lubricates them, inserts them in her pussy, and leaves the tampon-style string dangling outside for easy removal.
Good points: Inserted into the vagina, they are supposed to produce titillation while the woman walks around wearing them during the day.
Bad points: They don't. And they clank together, making people stare at you oddly on the bus. Oh, and sometimes they fall out.
Rating: 1/10. No clitoral stimulation to speak of, so really only suitable for girls who enjoy the idea of smuggling drugs through Customs.

The Virgin

Slogan: 'An amazing lifelike vibrating pussy that is guaranteed to provide hours upon hours of pure orgasm delight. Made in China.'
Price: £29.99
How it works: You plug in the batteries, do roughly the same with your old fella, and then lubricate it before thrusting.
Good points: As it's fitted with its own hymen, you at least know that nobody else in the shop has used it already. It's made of very soft rubber, and it fits in your hand so you can 'assist' the vibrations by masturbating normally.
Bad points: It is possibly the vilest colour in creation. And it really smells of rubber. I mean *bad*.
Rating: 4/10. Put it this way: you might have sex with it, but you're not going to fall in love.

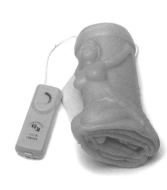

French Tickler

Slogan: 'Zür stimulation der Frau während des Sex' (Whatever the *hell* that means).

Price: £3.99

How it works: Worn around the base of the penis to provide gentle contact with her clitoris.

Good points: The stretchy rubber is pretty easy to put round your shaft, and once on it will help you maintain a full erection. The soft, dimpled pad will rub against her clitoris during sex, leaving your hands free to explore other parts of her body.

Bad points: Looks a bit stupid. Won't work if you're doing doggy style.

Rating: 9/10. It really does keep her turned on.

Cucumber

Slogan: 'Lovely Qs! Two fer a pahnd!'

Price: 50p

How it works: Like a dildo.

Good points: She can leave it lying round the house without arousing any suspicion. It's cheap, she can pick the size she likes and, after a good wash, it can be turned into sandwiches. How many other sex toys can you say that about?

Bad points: It can break if you wield it too vigorously, requiring you to then probe about inside her like a character from *All Creatures Great and Small*. Some women prefer a corn-on-the-cob, because the added girth and ridges apparently give more pleasure. And like any kind of foodstuff, whether it's Mars Bars or bananas, you have to warm it up to room temperature first or she'll howl like a cat that's been jabbed with a compass.

Rating: 7/10. A sex aid that's probably as old as agriculture itself. But none the worse for that.

Furry Cuffs

Slogan: 'Stay close to the one you love.'

Price: £9.99

How they work: You've seen *Cagney & Lacey*...

Good points: Sturdy enough for most bondage games, but with a nice fur-lined exterior that cuts down on bruises.

Bad points: A bit poncy if you want to act out a proper 'Dungeon Master' fantasy.

Rating: 9/10. A friendly, lightweight way to introduce your girlfriend to the idea of bondage.

149

Little Beaver Double Tickler

Slogan: 'Have twice the excitement!'

Price: £3.99

How it works: Secured at the base of your shaft, it simultaneously caresses her clitoris and burrows inside her arse.

Good points: Works on the same principle as a French tickler, except it's battery-powered and has an extra 'anal probe'. Ideally, this means she can combine the fun of normal sex, backdoor sex and a vibrator all at the same time.

Bad points: The battery box hangs off your penis, and if you try anything too athletic it starts to swing around like Tarzan on a jungle vine. Also, the head of the clitoral stimulator is modelled on a beaver. This is not attractive.

Rating: 7/10. Certainly offers a few new angles, but you have to line everything up again between thrusts.

Penis Extension.

Slogan: 'Be bigger — now!'

Price: £20.50

How it works: It slips over the top of your penis, and is best held in place with a condom.

Good points: Makes your cock seem a few inches bigger. Duh.

Bad points: Covers your glans, so it seriously cuts down on your own pleasure. And if you ever split up with your girlfriend, there are going to be plenty of 'Lilliput' gags about you doing the rounds.

Rating: 1/10. If she really wants something more filling under the duvet, use a dildo or strap-on to warm her up.

Electric Razor

Slogan: 'So good I bought the company.'

Price: £40 plus

How it works: Take an ordinary 'three-head' electric razor, remove the blades, and use it to massage her erogenous zones.

Good points: Costs nothing if you already own one. And it's surprisingly effective at getting her warmed up.

Bad points: You have to make sure you clean it really thoroughly beforehand. And afterwards.

Rating: 5/10. You'll probably get good marks for invention, but don't expect it to work half as well as a vibrator.

Cock Mould.

Slogan: 'Clone your bone.'

Price: £20

How it works: A bit like making your own candles, except you have to maintain a full erection for the three minutes it takes the wax to dry. You insert your member into the casting mix tube, choose one of five colours to immortalise yourself in, and then wait for it to set. The result? A handy, highly personal memento for your girlfriend to enjoy when you're away travelling.

Good points: It's a personal touch, so she might even be thinking of you when she uses it. And you can cheat and make it look bigger, thus enhancing your reputation among her friends.

Bad points: You need to have some artistic flair, or at least a Pottery 'O' level to get it right. Or else it looks more like an Easter Island statue than a penis.

Rating: 6/10.

Ribbed Condoms

Slogan: 'Add a little spice to your love-making.'

Price: £3.99 for three

How they work: You know already.

Good points: The ribs are supposed to add stimulation to the vagina when fucking.

Bad points: Well, my ladies said they couldn't notice much difference, except when the cock was rubbed against the clitoris from outside as part of foreplay.

Rating: 3/10. These aren't going to make you any more of a stud, so save your cash and go for the simpler model.

Anal-Beads

Slogan: 'A new development from the Orient.'

Price: £3.99

How they work: They stimulate the male G-spot and/or the anus of both genders.

Good points: Either of you can wear them. When pulled out swiftly at the point of orgasm, they certainly make you go 'Wow!'

Bad points: Even if well-lubricated, it's no walk in the park to insert them up your anus. Timing the pull with your climax requires concentration. And you *really* want to make sure you've wiped them properly before using them, or there could be an embarrassed silence after sex.

Rating: 5/10. If you enjoy a finger up your bum, then these are for you. If not, steer clear, or you'll know what it feels like to be the fairy on top of a Christmas tree.

Toy of Joy

Slogan: 'Soft, sensual, sensational!'

Price: £21.99

How it works: You smear a healthy dollop of lubricant around the lips, crank up the power, and make love.

Good points: When applied to the sensitive bell end region, it does give you a new and exciting buzz.

Bad points: Unfortunately, once you start thrusting, your cock ends up in the useless 'wind sock' area at the back, leaving the vibrating part around the insensitive base of your cock. And it looks more like Noel Edmonds's beard than any vagina I've seen.

Rating: 3/10. If you can get over the mental trauma of feeling like Jeffrey Dahmer playing with a surgically removed body part, this will get you to orgasm eventually. But, at these prices, it's a long ride for a short slide.

Clitofing

Slogan: 'Make your woman ready for love in no time.'

Price: £4.50

How it works: You slip the latex 'thimbles' over your fingertips and stroke her pussy in the usual way.

Good points: It's cheap, and the basic principle is sound, though my jury was out on whether it actually feels any nicer than normal flesh.

Bad points: You look as though you've got a particularly nasty skin disease. And it certainly doesn't make it 'easier to have simultaneous orgasms', as the packaging claims.

Rating: 2/10. Stick to normal handwork.

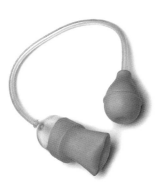

Oro-Simulator

Slogan: 'Strokes up and down your penis . . . all by itself!'

Price: £18.99

How it works: You roll the latex collar over your cock and pump air in and out of the plastic dome. This makes it bob up and down, allegedly like a woman's mouth.

Good points: The picture on the box is very funny.

Bad points: It goes up and down, sure, but there is no way it feels like a blow job. And pumping the bulb is more tiring than having a normal wank would be.

Rating: 0/10. Utterly absurd.

Taking Care of Your Sex Toys

A sex aid may not be the most expensive purchase you ever make, but it will require a lot more care than many of the items lying around your home. This is especially true if you have multiple partners and intend to use your toys on more than one of them.

Cleaning is the most obvious necessity, and you should wash them after each use. Soap and water may be enough to get rid of any stray pubic hairs and bodily fluids, but from a hygiene point of view it's better to use alcohol or a ⅐th solution of bleach. Dry them away from direct heat, as this may prematurely age or crack the rubber.

Also, here's a handy tip if you've got a vibrator in your armoury. When you first open it, the battery compartment will contain an instruction leaflet. Instead of throwing this away, leave it curled up inside. It will lessen the rattling noises when you put the bad boy to good use.

The Real Doll

You may have noticed in the last section that I didn't mention any blow up dolls as possible sex aids. This is because I am firmly convinced that they're crap. Even the most up-market designs have the faces of escaped lunatics, the sex appeal of a hot water bottle, and pubic hair that is even less realistic than Brucie's toupee.

Fortunately, science may soon make up for these low standards. By adapting the techniques used in animatronics (most commonly seen in Hollywood movie special effects), an American company has come up with the 'Real Doll'. Completely solid and built around a steel skeleton, it has silicone breasts, teeth and private parts; it has fingers and limbs that can be moulded into any position that a normal woman could manage; it weighs eight stone; and customers can choose from a wide variety of features, ranging from nail colour to breast size, hair style to foot size, and facial type to lipstick colour. All the features are moulded from real models, so it actually looks fantastic.

Buying one costs — wait for it — £4,999, with this price rising to £5,249 if you want the Deluxe model, which also has an anal entry. Clearly, this is not chump change, but you do get your money's worth. Mind you, as the manufacturers plan to construct a doll in the near future that moves and talks as well as looking like a porn star, you might want to hang on for that . . .

Games

George Melly, the extremely fat jazzman, used to perform an amusing party piece. He would remove all his clothing, stand on a table in a crowded pub, gesture to his private parts and say 'Man'. Next, he would tuck them away between his legs and say 'Woman'. Then, as a climax, he would turn his baggy, corpulent arse to the audience and — with his genitals still poking back between his thighs — shout 'Bulldog!' As finales go, it certainly beat an encore of 'Is You Is Or Is You Ain't My Baby?', but as a game leading to sexual intercourse it has one major flaw. Because, while it's easy enough to take your own clothes off, the real trick is in getting other people to do it too.

Most of us, of course, will know this only too well from our adolescence. I can still remember, with the sort of Proustian clarity that only deep shame can guarantee, my first ever attempt to play 'Spin the Bottle'. It was after the annual disco at my Catholic boarding school, when my pal and I managed to sneak two girls back to his room. Once we'd impressed the ladies by smoking all their cigarettes and jamming along to 'Suspect Device' on our squash rackets, we decided the time was ripe to spice things up a bit. A bottle was produced. Forfeits were devised. But then . . . well, then things went rapidly downhill. The girls kept choosing 'truth' over 'dare', and in an effort to up the ante, I challenged my pal to run down the corridor with no clothes on. I figured that the sight of him slipping out of his brown John Conteh-style Y fronts would show the girls what heavyweight studs we were, but no sooner was he starkers than they were gathering their things and heading back to the disco, leaving us only with a wounding remark about 'virgins'.

This painful incident must have scarred me, because for years afterwards I took a very sneering attitude to sex games. They were strictly for lonely blokes who lacked the charm to chat up women properly. They were for losers. When I played poker, it was going to be for money, not underwear. (Mind you, when you consider the physical state of the guys I sit down with at the baize every Thursday,[4] this was perhaps an unsurprising decision.)

The more I've learnt about sex, however, the less sure I am of this superior attitude. After all, anything that encourages people to go to bed together can't be bad, and if games are played in the right spirit then the chances are they'll add an interesting and erotic twist to the occasion. The more complicated ones can even help you to discover the true extent of your partner's sexuality — and your own — whether they involve role-playing, swapping or an intoxicating element of risk.

And, anyway, they're a lot more fun than Ker-Plunk . . .

---

[4] And I refer here, in particular, to Adam 'Momo' Moses.

154

Balloon Jobs

Object: A superbly amusing ice-breaker, which can be played at large parties where the sexes are roughly equal in number. All the guys line up against the wall, put a balloon in their pants, and thread the nozzle through the front. The girls then kneel in front of a man each and start inflating the balloons. The first one to make it burst wins. You know, a prize or something.

Good points: Visually, a highly comic experience. And you'd be surprised how easy it is to guess which women are good at oral sex just from the puff and gusto they employ. Also, as it's essentially harmless, you can play it with a complete stranger rather than your sour-faced, disapproving partner.

Bad points: It hurts when the balloon pops. A lot.

Rating: Very much an hors d'oeuvre, as there's no guarantee this will get you anywhere near the business end of a duvet later. But it's still a great laugh.

Fish Sex

Object: In its purest form, this is a game where two of you make love while some friends watch. This isn't just for their titillation, however, but also for your safety, as to play it both you and your partner will need to be handcuffed with your wrists behind your backs. Thus handicapped, you wriggle about on the bed like fish, using only the flexibility of your bodies to screw.

Good points: If she's shy, then you can dilute this game by taking it in turns to be the fish, in which case you don't need an audience. Either way, it's extremely good exercise for your gut muscles.

Bad points: Only Harry Houdini could play this game and still look like a half-decent shag.

Rating: You'd have to be a pretty confident couple to do this. And you'd also have to trust your pals enough to unlock you afterwards, rather than take Polaroid photos and ransack your flat for jewellery and electrical goods.

Naked Lunch

Object: You draw lots and one person is chosen as the 'buffet counter'. They lie naked on a strong table and a selection of warm and cold foods are then laid out on their body. Everyone else then tucks in, using only their mouths, until the 'platter' is licked clean.

Good points: Agreeably messy and a lot of fun for all participants. Even more fun if you choose unusual sex foods — sucking strands of spaghetti off a girl's breasts is both nourishing *and* amusing.

Bad points: Sucking spaghetti off a *man's* privates may not be quite so much fun, but if sex games are to work properly, everyone has to go through with it.

155

Rating: So long as you a) choose your dinner guests carefully,[5] and b) avoid anything too hot, this sure makes a change from vol-au-vents.

Mazola Wrestling

Object: Like 'Seasons in the Sun' by Terry Jacks, this is an unforgettable classic from the 1970s. Californian swingers would lay down a tarpaulin, smear themselves with copious amounts of cooking oil, and then indulge in a spot of nude free-for-all wrestling.

Good points: Shy participants can wear a mask to disguise their identities, a bit like the grappler Kendo Nagasaki. And it's fun to slither about with loads of naked people.

Bad points: You need a huge shower curtain or the lining of a kid's paddling pool to make sure this one doesn't mess up your living room carpet. And everyone has to get in the shower afterwards, leaving your towels smelling of olive oil for weeks.

Rating: Like nude Twister, this one is more often talked about than played. But don't let that stop you. . .

Fantasy for Lovers

Object: Similar to Monopoly, in that it's a traditional board game which requires you to progress round a track by throwing dice and picking cards. Where it differs from Monopoly, however, is that instead of buying hotels on Mayfair you have to do stuff like take your clothes off and 'fondle your partner's breasts until she cries for you to stop'.

Good points: As the rules limit players to six items of clothing, it only takes about twenty minutes for everyone in the room to be naked. And the 'fantasy cards' make you do things which are amusing rather than gross, thus ensuring that frightened women don't run screaming from your house.

Bad points: The board is illustrated with photos of a very unattractive white naked bloke. With an afro.

Rating: This provided a hugely entertaining climax to a drunken dinner party, and I got to see my pal's date with no clothes on. But as I also had to stare at his cock for forty minutes, it's probably a game best played under strict 'mood lighting' conditions.

---

[5] *Suggested line-up: the girls of Hawaiian Tropic.*

Role Playing

Object: If *Give Us a Clue* was shown on the Red Hot Dutch channel instead of on BBC1, then this is roughly what it would end up like. Each participant draws a fantasy role from the hat and then has to spend ten minutes acting it out with total dedication. No excuses. No wimping out.

Good points: Easy to prepare. All you have to do is write down a selection of roles like 'Whore' and 'Vice Cop' on bits of paper, shuffle them up, and pick one each.

Bad points: Sometimes it backfires when you pick one of your own selections, and thus have to waste valuable time being 'a horny lesbian' or 'a virgin schoolgirl'. And you have to be really strict about doing the full ten minutes, or people start giving up before you've got anywhere.

Rating: If you've secretly always wanted to find out what your lover's real fantasies are, then this is the game for you. But if it transpires that she gets her kicks from golden showers or dressing you up in a nappy, don't blame me.

Ice Master

Object: Nothing to do with the huge bearded bloke who used to say 'I award the city of Cardiff fifty credits' on that show with Dani Behr, this is in fact one of the few diversions which can be played alone *or* in company. First off, you need some handcuffs, the key of which you attach to a piece of string, place in a bowl of water and then freeze in your icebox. If you're acting out a submissive fantasy alone, tie the string around your finger, close the handcuffs and lie there in bondage until the ice melts and you can free yourself. If your girlfriend's playing too, congratulations — you've just saved yourself the price of some string.

Good points: Adds a twist to her dominatrix act. And if you get bored, there's always the microwave. Or a hammer.

Bad points: As I found out to my cost, it's extremely hard to masturbate — or do anything at all — when you're padlocked to the bed. This could also prove highly embarrassing if your flatmate comes home from work early.

Rating: Although I quite like kinky games, this one didn't exactly rock my world. And it's quite uncomfortable unless you get those nice fur-lined bracelets.

Strip Poker

This game is the most popular 'swinging entertainment', which makes it all the more baffling that so many people have no clue how to play it. Some pathetic variations run along the lines of 'whoever gets a jack has to take off a sock', which completely gets rid of the skill element. I'm therefore taking it upon myself, a bit like the famous Edmond Hoyle (1672-1769), to set down the proper rules of this game. And although it can be played in any of the poker formats in use at Las Vegas casinos, varying from Texas Hold 'Em to Omaha to Baseball, I'm keeping it as five-card stud for reasons of simplicity. It works like this.

Each player receives one 'down' card (i.e. one that only he or she looks at) and one 'up' card which everyone can see. There is then a round of betting, started by the person with the highest up card showing. He or she must wager one item of clothing. Anyone who folds their hand must remove one item of clothing, but those who elect to stay in may 'call' the bet or raise it. Raises are limited to whatever is on the pot — e.g. if two people have already bet one item of clothing, the third person may only call that bet and then raise the pot by its current total: e.g. three items. This continues as three more cards, each followed by a round of betting, are dealt out. By this stage, most people will have cut their losses as they won't want to risk losing too many clothes at one go, but if it comes to a showdown, the ascending order of precedence in hands is this:

High Card: No pairs, no runs, just five unconnected cards. If yours is the highest on the table, you win.
A Pair: e.g. Two 7s and three unconnected cards.
Two Pairs: e.g. Two kings, two 6s, and an unconnected card.
Trips: e.g. Three of a kind, and two unconnected cards.
Straight: Five cards in different suits, all in a run, e.g. 4, 5, 6, 7, 8. Straights can *not* go 'over the top', i.e. Q, K, A, 2, 3.
Flush: Five cards all in the same suit, in no particular order.
Full House: e.g. Three 10s and two 4s.
Four of a Kind: e.g. Four 2s and an unconnected card.
Straight Flush: Five cards in the same suit, all in the right order.

If you win a hand, you get to keep the clothes that the losers have removed, and you can bet these later in lieu of your own garments. Obviously, given the concealed 'down' card, there are good opportunities to bluff, so if you've got the nerve you can triumph even if you get dealt trash all night. The game ends when everyone is naked except for the winner, who is presumably buried under a large mound of lingerie and shoes.

Stag Parties

Of all the vows made when a couple get married, perhaps the most rigidly observed is the one taken by the groom's best friends: that they will do their utmost to sexually humiliate him on his stag night. As this book is about making love, however, I shall gloss over such merry pranks as chaining him naked to a seat on the Aberdeen express or removing his eyebrows with a razor blade, and stick to the ones which involve hired female performers.

The first thing to get right when booking such professional entertainers is to ask the agency for *exactly* what you want. The guys who answer the phone have heard it all before anyway, and if you get embarrassed and coy, you'll only end up disappointed later. The usual form is for two girls to do a 'double show', in which they each do a strip, and then return half an hour later to do a strip together. If you want this to involve some crazy dyke action or the use of sex toys, specify when you book.

The flat rate for this is between £150 to £200 per girl, depending on how good looking or liberated they are. (You can also specify the skin and hair colour of the strippers you book, and this won't affect the price.) Of course, most stag parties will want a little bit 'extra', and if you ask for this in advance then the agency will send girls who are up for intimate physical shenanigans. They can still say no, however, if they don't like the look of you, or if you are too rowdy. It also won't help your chances much if they're being asked to perform in a horrible back room at your local boozer, especially if you have decorated it by throwing up.

Once you have negotiated a fee with the girls, they will expect to be paid up front. This is fine, but make sure that they know precisely what you want, or they may try to welch on the deal halfway through. Keep it simple and straight: 'We'll pay you an extra £150 if you give everyone here a hand job' is fine; '£150 for hand jobs, then?' is open to misinterpretation on the number of men who will be receiving this pleasure. Again, the girls are professionals, so don't think they'll be offended by candour.

Although the girls may have a driver, he will not be expected to serve as a minder. Once the show begins, they will keep discipline themselves, and you should respect their wishes as much as possible if you want a good evening.

There are many reliable agencies around, but if I had to recommend one it would be David Charles (tel. 01442 264402), if only because they have been in business for over thirty years, which should settle any 'fly-by-night' worries you might have once you've paid in advance.

159

Strip Bars

Filipino Roulette

If your stag party involves a sit down dinner in a private room, then you might want to try this entertaining sex game. It works like this: as you and your chums are sitting at the table, the hired female performer crawls underneath and unzips everyone's flies. Then she starts to give one of you a blow job, while everybody else tries to guess who's receiving it. If you accuse someone, a bit like in Cluedo, and get it wrong, then you have to leave the table. If you're right, then they have to. Naturally, you can make all sorts of 'come faces' to try to fool people, or attempt to look unconcerned if you're actually the lucky one.

If you'd prefer something less likely to result in the groom having his testicles removed, without the benefit of anaesthetic, by his angry bride, then you could try going to a strip bar. To avoid rip-offs, it's best to steer clear of poky little basements, where the drinks are wildly overpriced and the cabaret girls have the hard-bitten mien of veteran whores. Instead, visit a ritzy lap dancing establishment. These tend to be clean, well-run and filled with genuinely sexy girls. The only variations are whether the girls perform naked or just topless, and whether they do 'lap' or 'tableside' dancing. (In the former, the girls will gyrate in your lap; in the latter they are supposed to keep a distance of three feet. But, frankly, they never do.) Each dance will cost you a flat rate of about £10, for which your lady of choice will strip and wriggle about in front of you, sometimes even in time to the music. If you're really miserly, you can time your purchase to coincide with a really long song, with the seven minute, twenty-eight second live version of 'Bohemian Rhapsody' being a perennial favourite among tight wads. And at the better joints such as my own favourite, Stringfellow's, the girls give a free dance every hour to encourage trade.

Of course, as the alcohol begins to take effect, you'll probably try to chat the girls up, but be warned that they are all business. They've heard every line that a drunken chancer can come up with, and they can be fired or fined if they go home with a customer. Sure, if you're a movie star or you're spending cash like a billionaire, it's not beyond the bounds of possibility that they'll arrange to 'join you at a party later', but this is a rare exception. Also, be careful not to touch them while they're doing their routine. Your job is to drink in their beauty, not lend a helping hand. A first offence will probably earn you a polite rebuke, but if you push it too far, large fat-necked men in dinner jackets will throw you out of the front door. Often without opening it first.

For a more exotic floorshow, you really need to go abroad. Thailand may be too far for most stag parties, but you can still have plenty of fun in relatively nearby cities like Amsterdam, Berlin and Barcelona. The last contains a famous club called the Bagdad, which lays on a live sex show featuring five women and three men, all of whom screw on the stage, occasionally dragging a hapless punter aboard to help them out. It costs about £30 a head and, while preserving the groom's fidelity more or less intact, it certainly gives you something to giggle about guiltily during the wedding reception.

Visiting a Brothel

Although God-botherers and governments have been trying to close them down for thousands of years,[6] the fact remains that there's at least one brothel in every town. Tolerated by the cops, who recognise that it serves a need in the community, and almost invariably featuring a red light in its exterior decor, there's a fair chance you may visit one at some point in your life. (After all, it can't just be Hugh Grant who keeps those girls in cheap jewellery.) If you don't know where you nearest one is, your best bet is to ask a local taxi driver.

When you arrive, you will probably be asked to pay a joining fee (around £5) and to sign a members' book. Any pseudonym will do, because they're not going to ask for ID, but I find it's always amusing to use the name of a teacher you hated at school. Or an Arsenal footballer. Next, you'll go into the bar area, where you can buy drinks which, although over-priced, won't cost much more than in a normal nightclub. In here there may be a stage where strippers will ply their trade, but your eyes should be concentrating on the other ladies present. It's a safe bet to assume that anyone female in attendance is up for hire, but if you're in any doubt just politely ask 'Are you doing business?' Alternatively, sit at the bar looking lonely and someone will approach you soon enough. If you don't fancy the girl who speaks to you, don't worry about hurting her iron-clad feelings — just ask her about the woman you *do* like. She'll introduce you.

Once you've struck up a conversation, steering clear of all that 'my wife doesn't understand me bullshit', enquire how much she charges for what you desire, be it a hand job, blow job, full sex or other service. She'll come up with a figure, but — as in a Middle Eastern bazaar — you should be prepared to haggle. In my experience, they'll settle for half what they wanted, especially if it's a slow night. For rough guidance, full sex with a good-looking prostitute in London should set you back no more than £100. On top of this, you may have to pay a fee for her to leave the brothel, which usually involves paying £40 for a bottle of champagne. If you're extraordinarily lucky, this may even *be* champagne.

The next decision you have to make is do you want to take her back to your place, or do you want to use one of the back rooms. It's probably safer to stay on their premises: any worries you may have about being filmed 'on the

---

[6] *I exclude, obviously, religions which worshipped the Supreme and All-Powerful Phallus God, a deity who — according to the evidence of cave paintings — bears a striking physical resemblance to a certain men's magazine sex columnist I could mention.*

job' through a two-way mirror are completely unfounded. Once there, you should specify that you will get an hour of her time, rather than just the three minutes it will take her to make you come. This way, you should squeeze in at least a couple of orgasms for your money.

The only things you really have to worry about now are:

● **Safe sex:** Although she will provide condoms, you are at liberty to use one of your own, and it's not a bad idea — given that she fucks about five different men a day — if you bring some of those extra strength ones along.

● **'Clipping':** This is the expression for being ripped off by a prostitute, an occurrence that is much more common with street walkers than in brothels. If it happens to you, your best bet is to put it down to experience, as the lady at fault will no doubt be protected by some men who a) have baseball bats, but b) are not technically connected with the American major leagues.

Prostitute Slang

While some of these terms for the sexual practices available at brothels have undoubtedly dropped out of common usage, they still offer useful and comic insight into the preferences of our Continental cousins:

A bit of Greek: As you'd expect from all those vases featuring naked young men wrestling, this is a euphemism for anal sex.

A bit of Dutch: Our free-thinking, pot-smoking chums from the Lowlands have lent their name to a spot of lesbian action.

A bit of Russian: A slightly more complicated manoeuvre from the lads in astrakhan hats, this is where a man buggers you while a woman fellates you at the same time. Nice.

A bit of Spanish: A simple pleasure to enjoy after throwing a goat from a belltower in a bizarre religious ceremony, this refers to a 'tit wank'.

A bit of Turkish: Really quite horrible, and no doubt utterly undeserved by the nation which brought us the Hagia Sophia and the shish kebab, this is where you come in a woman's mouth and then punch her in the face. But don't feel too smug, because there's always . . .

A bit of English: The spirit of the public school comes shining through with this perversion, where the punter pays to get his bottom smacked with a cane.

CHAPTER SEVEN
Advanced Sex

If you are able to perform all the techniques, moves and methods I've listed in the book so far, then congratulations, you're already a top class lover. Ex-girlfriends no doubt close their eyes and think about you while their new partners huff and puff uselessly on top of them; they dream wistfully about you on lonely moonlit nights; and they tell their pals that, despite your many appalling personal habits and poor grasp of social skills, you were certainly great fun at bedtime.

But for many guys, of course, that's simply not good enough. No, they want to be *legends* under the sheets. They want their exes to be so distraught when they're dumped that they never make love to anyone else again. In short, they don't just want to split up with a girl, they want to *put her in a convent*.

So, how do you become this extravagantly talented in bed? Well, there are two schools of thought. The first, more extreme one is what we might call 'the de Sade approach', and it involves throwing yourself willy-nilly into all manner of sexual weirdness. As each new kink becomes jaded, you move onto another, even more bizarre sexual pursuit, picking up fresh thrills as you go. While the good Marquis's writings prove that you will never run out of new things to experiment with — he advocates sex with anything from decapitated monkeys to barn owls[1] — they do show up a fundamental weakness in this philosophy. I'm referring to the Law of Diminishing Returns. Because, if all that's egging you on is the schoolboyish joy of breaking a taboo, then you'll never be satisfied. You may even end up doing stuff that's uncomfortably close to the edge. To demonstrate, check out this perverse end-result of taking things too far. Although hard to believe, and guaranteed to make any male readers clench their knees together in fright, it is quoted verbatim from an American medical journal:

'…one side effect of inserting objects such as toothpicks and wires into the urethra while masturbating is that some men tear the soft tissue inside. A small number then choose to insert a larger implement to stop these lacerations from healing, resulting in an overall expansion of the urethra. If this process is repeated using progressively larger objects, then they are able,

---

[1] *He does, however, draw the line at lawyers.*

over time, to produce an opening in the glans penis… which is *wide enough for another man to thrust his erect penis into*[2]. This aberrant simulation of intercourse is known as a meatotomy.'

Now I'm not suggesting you're going to rush straight out and try this, or even the bit with 'toothpicks and wires'. And I'm not going to condemn those residents of the San Francisco area who gave it a whirl either. Good luck to 'em, I say — my point is simply that this kind of thing is counter-productive. Getting too wild is going to make it harder to find a partner with whom you can achieve mutual satisfaction, rather than easier, so you'll get far less opportunity to show what a dynamite shag you are.

For this reason, I reckon it's better to sign up for the other school of thought. Although just as keen on experiment, it's a lot milder. As a basic rule of thumb, you stick to trying out stuff that you wouldn't be ashamed to tell your best mate about, things like anal sex, group sex and bondage, which — let's be honest — most of us have at least considered. Of course, you could still run up against a wall of refusal from your partner when you mention them, and she may even say something like 'It's wrong to make me try things I'm not happy with.'

I'm not going to argue with that, mainly because I already get enough hate mail from the various moustachioed trolls and hobgoblins who make up the feminist movement, but let us imagine for a moment that it's your girlfriend who suggests something kinky and *you* are the reluctant one. OK then, now I can speak my mind, and what it wants to say is this: 'Don't be such a pussy. You are part of a nation that conquered the world, the scion of a proud, intrepid people who stared danger in the face for a thousand years and never once flinched from the challenge. I daresay your ancestors didn't much want to battle against the stormy waves, fearsome Fuzzy-Wuzzies, parched deserts and pointy-hatted Krauts, but they did it all the same. *They gave it a go.* So at least have the bottle to try the routines I suggest in the rest of this chapter. If you don't like them, fine, at least you'll have shown the right attitude — the *only* attitude — that'll make you a complete and fearless lover.'

Oh, and we won the World Cup.

---

[2] *My italics. But yours for £9.99 if you buy the book.*

Anal sex

If done in conjunction with clitoral caresses, backdoor love can make your partner's orgasms even more intense, and for men it offers a tighter fit than the vagina and a thrill of 'naughtiness'. Needless to say,[3] in these days of grim communicable disease, scrupulous hygiene and the use of adequate protection are vital. The rectum does not usually contain any faecal matter, but it is home to all sorts of bacteria. If you get them in her pussy or your mouth, you could both come down with something unpleasant, so ensure that your hands and fingernails are clean, that you use a condom, and that you change this and wash thoroughly before switching your ministrations to her vagina. You should also note that the wall of the rectum is a lot more fragile than that of her muff, so go gently. Whether it's your finger or your cock that you're putting up there, let her ease back onto it rather than just ramming it home like a jackhammer. The positions suitable for anal love are pretty similar to the ones listed in the 'Rear Entry' chapter, but here are a few of the unique wrinkles it affords . . .

● **Going round the world:** Named in honour of Ferdinand Magellan, the first man to circumnavigate the globe,[4] this technique involves licking her ringpiece with your pointed tongue until it's well-lubricated, at which point you insert a finger. Then you twist it in and out in a delicate corkscrew motion, supplementing this with more tongue-work.

● **The anal clockface:** Imagine there's a clockface superimposed on her anus, with twelve o'clock pointing towards her vagina and six o'clock pointing towards her spine. By far the most sensitive clusters of nerve endings will be at two and ten o'clock, so concentrate your fingering on these parts. If you do it with your tongue, that's called rimming.

● **Felching:** One for the genuine pervert only, or for someone who just can't get enough zinc in their diet, this is where you come in her arse and then suck the semen out afterwards. Even if you use a straw, it's going to be messy.

● **Fisting:** I'm not going to describe full fisting (or 'punching' and 'handball' as

---

[3] Q: So why am I saying it? A: Because I get paid by the word.
[4] OK, that's not true. Everybody knows he had the 'soapy tit wank' named after him.

it is sometimes known), because it is mainly a homosexual practice.[5] But you can easily do a bantamweight version of this without having to emigrate to Southern California. Simply bunch your outstretched fingers and thumb into a point, lob on a dollop of lubricant, and ease all five of them into her anus. Once they're inside, you can open them out, and your girlfriend may find the 'yawning' sensation a great turn on. And if she doesn't, you can stop.

● **The double trigger:** A handy way to simultaneously caress her clitoris and anus.[6] You place the ball of your thumb on her clitoris, use your middle three fingers to stroke her perineum, and slide your wettened little finger up her tradesman's. Although trickier to do than most Masonic handshakes, this will actually give her multiple pleasures if you get the hang of it.

Anal Sex for Men

As someone far more interested in cooking than me once wisely remarked, 'What's sauce for the goose is sauce for the gander.' And so, if you're happy enough to penetrate your missus up the behind, it seems only fair that you should be prepared to give it a crack yourself. Specifically, *your* crack. Not only will this allow her to get some unique kicks by feeling a 'male' dominance in bed, but it will also let you find out how much fun a good seeing to is if all you can see is the pillow.

Start off by getting your lover to play with your anus during sex, perhaps inserting an oiled finger up to the first knuckle. If this excites you — and it's sometimes helpful to do it in conjunction with a blow job, rather than just 'cold' - encourage her to push the finger deeper. By this stage you'll know whether it freaks you out or drives you wild. If the former is true, then stick to normal sex and try to avoid serving any long prison sentences in the Istanbul area; if the latter is true, then you might want to work up to some of these methods:

● **Vibrator:** Get her to swirl it around your anus, directing the point especially on your 'ten and two o'clock' areas. Then, after applying plenty of K-Y or baby

---

[5] *Which is not to say that some of my best friends, etc . . .*
[6] *Both of whom, of course, went on to play deputies in* The Dukes of Hazzard.

oil, she can probe the first inch of it inside you. As your arse dilates, move to a thrusting motion, accompanied by handwork on your cock. If you enjoy the feeling but have any psychological 'shirtlifter' worries, use a plain white vibrator rather than the realistic cock type.

● **Strap on:** With one of these, you can actually have sex. She puts on a kinky, Emma Peel-style leather harness, which contains a steel ring through which a 'strap on' dildo can be fitted. These vary in size from a two inch butt plug to the sort of jutting prong that could intimidate a rhino. Start small, use plenty of lube, and adopt the all fours position. After a thorough fingering, ease your self back onto the dildo while she holds your hips — exactly as you would both do if the roles were reversed. Once you begin to fuck, it will teach you one valuable lesson: that sex for the recipient is more sensual and exciting if the person 'giving' is tender.

● **Double dildo:** One disadvantage of strap on sex is that, apart from a feeling of power, your lover will get no appreciable thrill from screwing you. Luckily, this can be solved by purchasing a 'double-header'. Used more often by lesbian couples seeking mutual penetration, in this instance your girlfriend puts one end of it inside her pussy, then feeds the free end between your cheeks. By rocking back and forth, you can thus have a one-off experience of mutual penetration, a bit like being that pushmi-pullyu animal in the Dr Dolittle books.[7]

S&M

Although I've spent quite a few evenings at dungeon parties and Torture Garden jamborees, I am not one of those people who find that there is 'a thin line between pain and pleasure'. From my point of view, in fact, there's a bloody enormous line between them. But, with equal conviction, I have to report that everybody else in attendance at these events, whether they were being whipped on the bare buttocks with heavy metal chains or having their stilettos licked by a kneeling gimp in SS fatigues, seemed to be having a whale of a time. It thus seems only reasonable to include some hints about injecting a spot of S&M into your own relationship.

---

[7] *Dr Dolittle is against animal testing. Except when their spelling needs a brush up.*

If you experiment with these and consequently find that they add real zap to your love life, you can easily find out about the harder, Spanish Inquisition stuff by buying a specialist magazine or visiting a shop that sells rubber gear. The helpful staff, usually distinguished by having enough bodypiercings to qualify for a seat on the Minerals Exchange, will point you in the right direction. In the meantime, there's no better way to dip your toe in these sometimes choppy waters than by trying out bondage.

● **How it works:** Although there's no reason why bondage cannot follow egalitarian principles, with each of you taking turns to be trussed up, the fact is that most couples soon find out who is the 'bottom' (submissive) and who is the 'top' (dominant). While it might sound a lot more fun to be the boss, it is in fact more often the victim who stands to gain the most pleasure from this arrangement. Being tied up will increase adrenalin, and thus the capacity for sexual excitement, and being 'helpless' removes any stress or performance anxieties from the act of making love. If your girlfriend ties you up, for instance, it's down to her to call the shots. She can tease you to the brink of orgasm numberless times, making your final climax that much more exhilarating. She will be refreshingly aggressive, and all you have to do is lie there and smile. On the minus side, bondage will inhibit the amount of positions you can do, and — obviously — you have to be in a very trusting relationship.

● **Tying up tips:** As you never know when the phone's going to ring or the gas man is going to pop by to read the meter, you should never tie your partner up with anything that can't be undone in 30 seconds. There are some handy 'quick release' knots illustrated on the right, but a good general rule is not to use anything which you would be reluctant to cut with scissors in an emergency. (So, while roping your lover with £50 Lanvin silk ties might seem the last word in sophistication, bear in mind that they're going to look pretty stupid snipped in half.)

Stockings and tights add a welcome kinkiness to proceedings, but they are a right bastard to untie, so avoid them unless you can afford to shell out for more. Instead, stick to rope (not string — it's too thin and will cut her) or ribbon, a roll of which can be bought inexpensively and used over and over again.

Finding somewhere to tie the other ends to is easy if you own a four poster bed, but let's face it, you don't. Futons are the best substitute, as you can pass the rope round the slats under the mattress, but if you have a modern bed

with a headboard, then you'll either have to use very long restraints or purchase some specialised 'spreader bars'. Equipped with leather cuffs, these rigid bars will keep her (or you) in an 'X' shape, ready for fun.

● **Blindfolds and gags:** As you get a little bit heavier in your sex play, you'll probably want to use these. In my experience, the best blindfolds to use are those free ones you get on long haul flights, which the cabin staff don't mind you stealing. Wear these,[8] and it will also require less imagination to combine bondage with whatever fantasy or role play you're into.

Gags require slightly more effort, as they are rarely given out to aeroplane passengers, even those travelling first class. You should avoid putting anything in the victim's mouth in case of choking, and it's also a good idea to steer clear of duct tape. Although easy to apply, it's painful to tear off once the fun is over. Stick instead to a silk scarf knotted around the back of the head, but remember that this will stop you having any oral action, and may interfere with . . .

● **Release words:** These are vitally important in any game that involves pain or restraint. Because, while it's undeniably true that phrases such as 'Oh God! No!' *can* mean 'For Christ's sake, don't stop!', either partner may seriously want to bring things to a halt. Thus, you need to establish a codeword beforehand that cannot be mistaken for a cry of ecstasy, something entirely removed from the regular argot of pleasure. ('Darren Day', for instance.) If she is going to be gagged, then the best alternative is to have her hold three coins in her hand during sex — if she drops these, it means 'stop at once'.

● **Pain:** There's more to enjoying S&M sex than being trussed up like a turkey, of course. The whole point is for there to be a certain transaction of pain. The milder forms of this include spanking, which can make the nerves tingle pleasantly and bring a rush of nostalgia to anyone who attended public school; biting and pinching; or flagellation. Unless you are both hardcore S&M artists, of course, this last feature should be kept at the pianissimo level, using a rolled-up pillowcase that will leave no marks on the skin, rather than the sort of cattle whip that can make an Aberdeen Angus change direction.

● **Dangers:** This kind of sex can be highly dangerous, so participants need to follow certain guidelines. The five most important ones are: don't tie anything

---

[8] *Although not both at once, unless your fantasy involves Mr Magoo having sex with David Blunkett.*

around the neck, or too tightly around arteries in the wrist; never truss someone face down or they might suffocate; never keep them tied up for longer than half an hour; release them immediately if limbs begin to 'go to sleep'; and never leave them alone.

Kinky sex

In the olden days they knew a thing or two about group sex. Chinese emperors of the T'ang dynasty, for example, enjoyed the services of 121 women: the empress herself, three consorts, nine wives of the second rank, 27 wives of the third rank, and 81 concubines. While this was undoubtedly a great ruse to guarantee a date on Saturday nights, it is sadly frowned upon in Bexleyheath nowadays.

Nevertheless, it is easily possible to find like-minded couples to join you and your partner under the duvet. *Desire* magazine (call 0171 627 5155 for details) is filled with small ads from swingers every month, and most of them are accompanied by a photograph so you know what you're getting. The real difficulty is persuading your other half that it would provide a fillip to your love life. You'll know whether this one is on the cards or not, but I always recommend a) asking her about her fantasies, and b) if one them involves three in a bed, inviting some friends round for dinner and getting them extremely pissed.

Once you have arranged the extra personnel, there is still some work to do. As you are playing with sensitive emotions like trust and jealousy, the whole line-up must agree what's going to happen, and what the limits are. Are you simply going to shag your own girlfriends in the same room, watching each other? Are you going to swap partners? Is there going to be any same-sex action? Are you all going to roll around in a giant ball of limbs and sexual apertures? After these parameters have been set, here are some ideas for the appropriate positions.

● **The doggy loop:** This is the perfect method if you're lucky enough to end up in bed with two women. One of them lies down on her back with her legs open. The other rests on all fours above her, facing the other way as though they were doing a 69. You then penetrate the second girl in doggy style. As you screw, the first girl can lick your balls as they shuttle back and forth. For everyone to be happy, it's best if the women have Sapphic tendencies, because they can also go down on each other simultaneously while you thrust.

● **The toss for ends:** If the line up is limited to one girl and another bloke, you may want to be more circumspect. After all, performing in close proximity to a man with a raging hard-on may unsettle you, especially if a) he's better hung than you, or b) you think he may have gay intentions. Your safest bet in this case is to stick to opposite ends of the lucky woman, with one of you enjoying some oral action, and the other sticking to the pussy. If the sight of someone's penis freaks you out, then once again your best bet is to stick to doggy style. This will pretty much mask things.

● **The double penetration:** If you're free-wheeling enough not to have such panics, then you can give the girl an unforgettable 'DP' (double penetration) fuck. She lies on her side, and one of you adopts the Spoons position, screwing her in the arse. The other fellow lies in front of her and penetrates her pussy. It's best to take things very slowly at first until you are sure of the right rhythm, and bear in mind that you will inevitably experience a certain amount of 'ball banging'.

● **The square:** If you and your lover are entertaining another couple, and assuming you have a big strong bed, then you can limit 'infidelities' to kissing by adopting this position. Your girlfriend lies on her side with her legs open, and you penetrate her at right angles. On the opposite side of the bed, your guests mimic this in such a way that your mouth is next to his girlfriend's, and vice versa. This has all the advantages of group sex with the added bonus that you can assure each other that 'nothing really happened more than a snog' afterwards.

● **The Mongolian clusterfuck:** This is full-blown group sex, and only for the confident. Expect a lot of swapping: there is absolutely no chance of remaining faithful to one another. As in the 'Doggy Loop', the girls lie on top of each other, but now there are two men present, one stationed at either end. They alternate between screwing and being sucked, and change ends whenever the mood takes them. Normally, the excitement gets too much and this delicate position collapses into an untidy heap, in which anarchic state anything goes.

Sex tricks of the famous

Famous men and women are usually at pains to avoid gossip about their sexual practices appearing in print, but this doesn't stop salacious nuggets of information leaking out. Many of the best rumours — e.g. that Catherine the Great shagged a horse, or that the Emperor Tiberius had slave boys who would nibble at his genitals when he went swimming — are neither true nor practical for today's lovers, but there are still some that might be worth the effort of recreating.

● **Peter Andre's Fizzer:** The muscular Australian singer, once popular with teenage girls, has a particularly novel method for guaranteeing that his girlfriends reach orgasm. It works like this: once you have warmed your lover up to the brink of a climax with foreplay, you take an Alka Seltzer tablet, break it in half, crumble off any sharp edges, and gently place it about 3 inches inside her vagina. Now continue masturbating her. After a few seconds, the pill will begin to tingle and froth, and then she'll start to feel a slight burning sensation. Let her squirm until this becomes almost unbearable, at which point you slide an ice cube inside her too. The soothing relief apparently ensures that she'll be convulsing and yelping with joy.

● **Madonna's candlewax:** As seen in a rather crap movie she starred in,[10] this is a lightweight S&M trick that anyone can try. When your lover is tied up, you take a lighted candle and drip the melting wax onto her skin. It hurts for a second before cooling, but — unlike many other S&M practises — it leaves no permanent scars. It's also easy to scratch off with a fingernail afterwards.

● **Bill Clinton's cigar dildo:** While one has to doubt the leadership capabilities of a man who can mistake a vagina for a humidor, this trick apparently gave great pleasure to the goon from Little Rock. As advertised in the Starr Report, you insert a cigar into your lover, wettening its end with her juices, and then smoke it later. In this form it's unlikely to do any harm, but you should refrain from any serious thrusting because the tobacco leaf may shred inside her pussy, leaving fragments of nicotine which will irritate the vaginal walls. Oh, and don't try it with anything less plutocratic than a Romeo y Julieta — she's going to look silly with a Marlboro Light inside her.[11] And you're going to look cheap.

---

[10] *Although that doesn't really narrow it down much, I agree.*
[11] *I award myself a Pulitzer Prize here for avoiding any jokes about Camels.*

Genital piercing

Although you might think that genital piercing is a relatively new phenomenon, popular only among tedious young people wishing to display their 'individuality' to an uninterested world, it is in fact a very ancient practice stretching back to the Romans and Egyptians. Nowadays, however, there is a far greater variety of 'jewellery' available, and thanks to medical advances it is much safer to adorn your body.

Modern piercings range from septum spikes to facial horns, but we'll concentrate on those sited in the genitals. This isn't to say that they enhance sexual pleasure — indeed, once the skin around them has 'settled down', they have almost no effect at all on physical enjoyment. (The thrill is more psychological — the pervy feeling of having a new toy to play with.) Only piercings on the tongue or lips have any real erotic value: when applied to the private parts during cunnilingus or fellatio these can add a different texture to proceedings.

If you're considering having one inserted, make sure your professional uses Implant Grade Surgical Stainless Steel, and avoid sexual activity for six weeks after the fitting. If you try any hanky panky before that, there's a good chance you'll end up with a nasty infection.

● **Foreskin:** Obviously only available to those of us who dodged the Rabbi, these piercings were originally designed to enforce chastity. Two holes were made in the foreskin, and a small padlock could be attached, stopping the wearer from getting an erection. These days, however, rings and bars are for decoration only, and will roll back with the rest of your skin when you get wood.

● **Ampallang:** This is a horizontal piercing through the head of the cock, and it gets its curious name from a tribe in Borneo.[12] Two round ball fittings close the ends of the barbell, making it smooth enough to be worn during sex. It's suitable only for circumsised guys, as the foreskin can bend it off course during the healing period.

● **Shaft:** It is possible to have a barbell fitted right through the middle of your penis. However, as this involves a lot of luck to avoid puncturing the urethra and veins, and will keep the tissues of the shaft anchored when they want to

---

[12] *They also came up with the advertising slogan 'Go to work on an egg'.*

expand to house an erection, it is really inadvisable. A safer bet is to
have rings or barbells knitted simply through the outer skin of the
cock. As with any penis modification, these have to be monitored to
make sure there are no loose or sharp parts showing before sex is
engaged in.

● **Implants:** Balls, usually made either of metal or pearl,
can be buried under the skin to give the penis a nubbly
surface. This will stimulate the vagina during sex, but there
is a danger that they will have to be 'massaged' back into
place after each encounter.

● **Prince Albert:** The number one favourite piercing among
men, this is rumoured to have been brought into fashion during
Victorian times, when guys used to tie back their cocks with ribbon
so they wouldn't show an offensive bulge in public.[13] The entry is
made on the underside of the penis, emerging at the bottom of the
urethra. Although users claim that it in no way interferes with sex,
there is one disadvantage: it can ruin your aim when pissing,
sending out a fan shape rather than a nice steady stream. In short,
get one of these and you've got the choice of sitting down in the
khazi or going to the dry cleaners a lot.

● **Dydoe:** A junior version of the ampallang, this is a barbell with
two round ends fitted through the skin of the glans. As it is quite
small, it's not uncommon for men with 'steel fever' to have more
than one inserted.

● **Scrotum:** The loose skin of the scrotum is easy to pierce, and the
most common decoration is a ring. Or several. Deep piercing should
be avoided, however, as it may damage or infect the testicles.

● **Guiche:** The furthest away from your cock, this piercing can
nevertheless be very painful if your job involves sitting down a lot.
It usually takes the form of a bar, inserted sideways through the
perineum, and fans claim it can enhance their pleasure if it's gently
tugged upon near orgasm.

---

[13] *With the notable exception of Anthony 'How d'you like them* apples' *Trollope.*

● **Inner labia:** The most common female piercing, because the skin here is relatively thin and so heals easily. The popular choice is either for a ring or barbell, and it's usually worn high up (i.e. nearer the navel) so it doesn't cause pain when the owner is walking.

● **Outer labia:** Because the skin tissue is thicker, this will take longer to heal and is more likely to get infected early on. Barbells are more often used than rings, because they cause less discomfort.

● **Clitoral hood:** Piercing the 'foreskin' or hood of the clitoris is much safer than messing with the clitoris itself, and the thin tissue lends itself to studs, barbells or rings without much pain.

● **Clitoris:** This can cause a lot of agony, especially if the woman has a small clitoris, as the piercing may chafe her where she's most sensitive. In some cases, it can even cause the jewellery to be forced to the surface of the skin and be rejected.

CHAPTER EIGHT *problems and solutions*

So far, this book has been all about making your sex life better, and — with the possible exception of that bit about wrapping cotton wool around your penis to make it seem thicker — there's a good chance it may have succeeded. But, let's be honest, love is a thing that can go wrong. And it never gets much worse than when you catch some hideous disease.

If this happens to you, it's essential that you visit your local Genito-Urinary Clinic as soon as possible. Of course, it is going to hurt a bit when the staff shove a spatula down your Jap's eye, and you'll probably suffer a bit of embarrassment too, but while I can suggest nothing cleverer than a bottle of Jim Beam to numb the pain, I am able pass on one handy tip for feeling less of a social leper. It's simple — wear a white coat. If you do this, the other losers in love in the waiting room will assume you're a doctor, and blushingly avoid your gaze.

As it may also give you a crumb of comfort to know what's ailing you before you see the cock doc, here's a brief rundown of the symptoms and remedies for the most common complaints . . .

Gonorrhoea

How you get it: Having unprotected sex with a fellow victim.

The symptoms: Between two and seven days after a sexual encounter, you begin to experience pain when taking a leak. And you notice a yellowy discharge coming out of your cock.

The cure: Hats off to Alexander Fleming, because penicillin usually kicks this one into touch.

General remarks: Thankfully pretty rare these days, unless your girlfriends ply their trade down at the docks.

Herpes

How you get it: From unprotected sex if she's got genital herpes, or from receiving a blow job if she has cold sores on her mouth.

The symptoms: Paint a big red 'X' on the door, because this is a bad one. Anything up to three weeks after being infected, tiny but horrible sores will begin to burst through on the skin of your penis and scrotum. These last for ages, and the side effects include muscle aches and mild feverishness. Although

they disappear, they won't quit: you'll have successive outbreaks (usually lasting about five days), and they'll be more likely to reappear if you're stressed at work or you've been caning the booze too hard.

The cure: No dice. Ever. But you can buy various creams that'll help you manage the problem. And once each attack is completely over, you're highly unlikely to infect a clean partner.

General remarks: You've got to be honest about this one, or your lover is going to be hiring some tasty blokes to beat seven shades out of you. And who could blame her?

Crabs

How you get them: From sexual contact, or even just sleeping in the same sheets as a sufferer.

The symptoms: These mothers really itch, and you'll feel like tearing your flesh until it bleeds.

The cure: Forget any old jokes about using a Philishave and a hammer — just pop down to the chemist and buy some cream. (If you're embarrassed, say it's for scabies — they use the same stuff.) Smother it on and laugh while your crustacean pals come face to face with chemical warfare. In your pants.

General remarks: No, you don't have to shave your pubes off.

Trichomoniasis

How you get it: Unprotected vaginal sex.

The symptoms: There may be none at all, but if you pass it on to a woman, she's going to get nasty, pus-coloured emissions from her muff. And there aren't chocolates enough in Belgium to make up for that one.

The cure: Antibiotics and a week of celibacy.

General remarks: You probably won't know you've got this one until your girlfriend looks at you sheepishly one day and says 'Erm… I've got something to tell you.' Be magnanimous (after all, *you're* not going to feel much pain) but use the moral high ground it affords you to your advantage.

Genital warts

How you get them: Having vaginal or anal sex.

The symptoms: The incubation period can last for years, so you'll probably never know who gave you these. When they arrive they'll look, as advertised, like warts, and they'll pop up on the skin of your penis, usually around the glans. They don't hurt and they're not terribly obtrusive, but anyone giving you

head with their eyes open is sure to notice them.

The cure: Three to choose from here: they can either be frozen off, burnt off, or daubed with an acid that'll make 'em shrivel away. However, once the virus is in you, it can re-occur at any time.

General remarks: The good news is that they usually don't reappear for years. The bad news is that millions of people in the UK have already got the HPV virus responsible.

Chlamydia

How you get it: Unprotected vaginal sex.

The symptoms: Slight pain on urination, perhaps a mild discharge. This one is actually quite hard to spot because the 'special effects' are so minor.

The cure: Antibiotics.

General remarks: It's important that your partner gets treated at the same time, otherwise you'll be passing chlamydia back and forth to each other like a ping-pong ball.

Cystitis

How you get it: The urethra gets infected with germs and becomes sore, often as a result of over-vigorous sex. Although mainly one for the ladies, blokes can come down with this too.

The symptoms: Pain when you pee.

The cure: Go to the chemist. Take the pills. And drink a lot of water.

General remarks: 50 per cent of women suffer from this at one time or another, so don't feel too sorry for yourself.

Thrush

How you get it: If she gets an imbalance of candida, a natural yeast in the vagina, she can pass it on to you.

The symptoms: Bad news at the urinal again. And your partner may experience both swelling inside the pussy and a discharge that looks a bit like cottage cheese.

The cure: There's strong evidence that eating 'live' yoghurt will help restabilise things, but it's quicker to ask your friendly pharmacist for a course of tablets.

General remarks: She's going to be hurtin' a lot worse than you are, so lay on the sympathetic cooing with a heavy trowel, eh?

Drugs and sex

It is always difficult for an author to write about drugs, especially if he doesn't want his book to be taken off the shelves, but I reckon I can get away with it so long as I limit my discussions to the effect they have on sexual performance. Mind you, as nearly every glassy-eyed hedonist who enjoys a toke, a snort or a sniff ends up trying to have sex, often going so far as to chat up furniture and pot plants, this won't exactly narrow things down. Nevertheless, I should say that in my considered judgement, sex is so good on it's own that you'd be wasting your time and money if you shell out on drugs to make it better. Not only can they mess up your performance and — in the case of hallucinogens — turn your partner into the Purple-Seven Breasted Monster With Sharp Teeth In Her Private Parts, but they'll probably have been cut with anything from talcum powder to rat poison by your avaricious dealer. And so, now that my knighthood's safe, let's take a peep down the microscope…

Alcohol
Pros: As you can buy it from any supermarket, you don't have to invite that boring bloke who wears shades indoors and insists on being referred to as 'the man' to your parties. It lessens inhibitions, making you feel sexier, and it reduces sensation, helping premature ejaculators to last longer in bed.
Cons: Getting the dosage right is key, as too much booze will lead to the inability to get or maintain a full erection. Add to this a familiar drop in quality control when it comes to selecting a partner, and the fact that you won't necessarily remember the sex the next morning.

Marijuana
Pros: Like alcohol, this can cut back your inhibitions, making you feel a lot more open and experimental in the sack. You become really aware of your skin and your nerve endings, and pleasure tends to come in longer, more mellow waves. And, hot news straight from the laboratory, grass can increase levels of phenylethylamine in the blood, a neurotransmitter associated with that part of the brain that controls love and lust. So you'll feel sexier.
Cons: It makes you talk shit. It makes you hungry. It makes you want to be very lazy in bed.

181

Morally righteous cautionary tale, included just in case I ever want to stand for the Conservative Party.

On 3rd June 1988, *The New York Times* ran a harrowing news item about a man who squirted a solution of cocaine into his urethra, as part of an attempt to enjoy sex even more. Although he was able to play 'the beast with two backs'[1] with his girlfriend, he afterwards found that his erection would not go down. This state of affairs lasted for three full days before he sought medical help, and once admitted to hospital he developed blood clots on his genitals, arms, legs, back and chest. After a fortnight on the ward, doctors discovered that gangrene had taken hold, and he ended up having both legs, nine fingers and his penis amputated. So remember, kids, just say 'no'.

[1] *And, in this instance, a bad case of the munchies.*

Ecstasy

Pros: You feel as though your entire being was designed to adore people, so sex tends to be characterised by lots of foreplay and affection. Your partner will seem like the most wonderful, sexy person alive, and you'll have fewer doubts about your own body or performance.

Cons: It can be dangerous, even fatal, especially if the drug has been watered down with impurities to boost the dealer's profits. You feel pretty spaced out and hungover for about 24 hours after a session.

Cocaine

Pros: You feel like a stud who could perform all night long. Suffused with a bogus sense of omnipotence, you'll want to try all sorts of kinky stuff that you'd otherwise be too shy to mention.

Cons: Cocaine makes it much harder to achieve climax, and it also makes your cock feel less rigid than usual. Plus, no matter how good the sex is, part of your brain will always be thinking 'I want to stop doing this and bang some more of that charlie.' And if you start thinking that pleasuring your nose is more fun that pleasuring your penis, I reckon it's God's way of telling you to stick to the tonic water and Cheese Footballs next time you go for a big night out.

Speed

Pros: Amphetamines give you a rush, making your senses feel more alive and quickening your heartbeat. You also feel like you have more stamina for the job in hand.

Cons: Although shagging like a demon is no problem, it can be hard to actually reach orgasm. So now you know what a woman feels like, eh?

Poppers

Pros: When inhaled, amyl nitrite causes a feeling of euphoria as the blood vessels in the brain dilate and the heart rate increases. This can make sex seem more urgent and exciting.

Cons: Like all drugs, you soon build up a tolerance to it, meaning that you have to up the dosage each time to recreate the best effects. Use can lead to nausea, headaches and fainting, and it's really perilous to anyone with heart problems.

Q&AS

It would be impossible for a writer to cover every aspect of sex in just one book. I don't say this out of false modesty. I don't say it as a veiled criticism of other sex authors. I don't even say it because it vastly increases the chances that HarperCollins will commission me to knock out a lucrative sequel to this volume. It just happens to be true. Nevertheless, over the years I've spent in the business, hundreds of men have written to me with queries, and here are my replies to some of the most common ones. I hope they'll provide the answers to whatever may be still be worrying you…

Do women like "good and hard" sex, or should I always be gentle and loving in bed?

The straight answer is "yes, they do like to be taken roughly". Hell, sometimes they just like to be bent over the sofa, have their knickers pulled down and be given a brisk seeing to without any foreplay at all. Because, while this kind of shag may not be so likely to guarantee them an orgasm, it does feel more earthy, primeval and lustful than a hour or two's lingering love-making. However, a woman's sexuality is a contrary thing, and it's not always easy to know what sort of sex she's in the mood for. The best advice I can offer you is to suggest that you and she develop a series of flirty signals, or that — if she ain't shy — she just whispers what she wants to happen in your ear. If she *is* apeshit for the rough stuff, then the best positions to choose are doggy, straight missionary or anything with her ankles on your shoulders and her pussy at your mercy. Avoid asking her to go on top, because this is one occasion where you have to do all the caveman thrusting.

When is the best time to have sex?

A woman's sexual nerve endings are at their most sensitive midway through her menstrual cycle. As for guys, their testosterone levels tend to be highest at around 9am every morning. Put these figures together and you have the recipe for an amazing shag at least once a month — so long as neither of you mind being late for work, of course.

183

I'm worried that my new girlfriend will dump me once we start having sex, because when my penis is erect it goes crooked. How did it get this way, and what can I do about it?

There are two possibilities here. Either you have a slight genetic fault in the trouser area, or you're suffering from Peyronie's disease, a painful disorder often caused by a trauma to the penis. Short of surgery, there's not much you can do about the first option, but if your erections are indeed accompanied by pain, then the good news is that Peyronie's usually corrects itself without treatment. That said, a bent cock shouldn't stop either of you having a good time in the sack, and may even add character to your performance. After all, during the recent Bill Clinton — Paula Jones legal scuffle, it was said that the President had "a distinguishing characteristic in his genital area — namely a bend", and he seems to get plenty of action.

Why do I fancy blondes more than other girls?

Men are attracted to blonde women on a subconscious level, because they say 'young and fertile' to our brains. For instance, if you look at a baby, it's very likely to have blonde hair and blue eyes, even if those colours will change completely as it matures. As men, we have a biological targeting mechanism which compels us to seek out a female we can breed successfully with, and the younger a woman appears, the more likely she is to bear us many children. It's the same reasoning behind the fact that most women, when surveyed, will say they fancy dark-haired men — because they seem more mature, and thus better fitted to the job of being a good provider.

When I make love to my girlfriend, she makes a lot of flatulent noises, although not from her arse if you get my meaning. How can I get her to stop this?

Vaginal wind is caused by air being pushed in by your cock as it 'trombones' between her labia. As this can only happen if your cock is too small to touch the sides of her pussy, however, I suggest you don't complain about it too much. Or too publicly.

Does a woman need to have an orgasm to enjoy sex fully?

In the long run of a relationship, things like trust and affection are much more important to both sexes than knockout orgasms every time you go to bed. But, that said, women have just as much right to expect a climax as men. Of course, there will be times when they don't feel like having one, or they're too tired, or their minds are on other things, in which case they'll probably be happy to miss out on the fireworks, especially as women don't find sex without an orgasm anything like as frustrating as guys do. The only real worry emerges if she's having lots of regular sex but still not coming. Arousal causes blood flow to her pelvic region, and if she is left unsatisfied this will take hours to seep away, leading in some cases to backache, sleeplessness and an unpleasant swollen feeling. If you can't make her come, you should a) learn how, or b) encourage her to masturbate to orgasm after sex.

I know that a merkin is a pubic wig. But what I can't understand is why anybody would need one. What's the reason?

In medieval days, part of the treatment for syphilis was to have your pubic hair shaved off. So as not to deter potential customers, prostitutes fashioned tiny syrups which they wore gummed abround their pussies. But don't worry, it mostly happened in France.

My sister told me that there's a surefire sexual technique for making women come, and it's called 'wibbling'. But she won't tell me the details. Is she having me on, or does it really exist?

Amazingly, wibbling is indeed a bizarre type of foreplay, although it's unlikely to make any girl achieve orgasm on its own. To do it, you go down on your girlfriend until she's wet, then use your fingers to gently stretch her vaginal lips to the side. Once they are at full extent, you let go, which results in a faint wibbling sound and apparently feels very nice for her. Nevertheless, as many women might object to being opened up like a bag of crisps, however pleasingly musical the result, it might be a good idea to ask whether she's up for it first.

As well as the G-spot, I've heard that women have something called the A-spot. Is this true?

Yes. It was discovered by accident when scientists were conducting tests to find a cure for vaginal dryness. Situated quite deep on the front wall of the pussy, about halfway between the G-spot and the cervix (that's the neck of the womb), when stimulated with the fingers it apparently made 75 per cent of the women feel extremely aroused. While the layman might wonder how much these doctors were getting paid to do their job, it's nevertheless something that can be usefully added to your compendium of sexual tricks. If you have long fingers, you should be able to caress it during foreplay — with light strokes or tiny figures of eight — and it can also come into play in those positions where the penis makes a lot contact with the front wall of the vagina. Rear entry is the best one.

I heard that the Chinese used to make love to their mistress's feet. Can this be true?

The cruel practice of 'foot-binding' began about 500 years ago in the Orient, and it results in the formation of deep, fleshy crevice under the arch — a 'Lotus Foot'. This was used very much as a second vagina, with the soft folds being penetrated by the penis, and there are many Chinese poems extolling the joys to be had in this way. Mind you, as they also thought it was cool to work on collective farms and ride crappy bicycles, I'd give it a miss if I were you.

Is it true that Coca-Cola is an effective spermicide?

A recent report by Harvard Medical School reported that the world's most popular fizzy drink is indeed used in some developing countries as a contraceptive douche. Subsequent laboratory experiments showed that it had a 91 per cent success rate in killing sperm. New formula Coke was less effective with a kill rate of 42 per cent, but Diet Coke was 100 per cent successful. But before you run for the fridge, I suspect that your lady friends would prefer it if you just wore a condom instead…

Why do I fall asleep right after sex?

Orgasm releases a chemical into the blood stream which encourages you to rest. This is quite normal, and you should take all those tabloid stories about pop stars doing it fifteen times a night with a pinch of salt. Anyway, once a night is enough for any woman, so long as you make sure she's well-satisfied before you come.

My girlfriend wants a photo of my penis to 'keep her company' when I go away on business trips. How can I make sure it looks good?

By 'good' I suspect you mean 'big', in which case I can suggest a few tips which might help you. Firstly, use a Polaroid camera, and holding it away from your body take a snap that only stretches from the navel to the knees. (This will stop anyone else identifying you, and put the kibosh on any Internet-style revenge she's planning if you ever dump her.) Secondly, when you pose for the photo, wear a white dressing gown and stand against a white wall. The gown will merge with the background, but the open sides of it will cover the outer edges of your legs, making them appear thinner. This in turn will have the effect of making your cock look thicker and bigger. Lastly, be sure to tease yourself into semi-tumescence before pressing the shutter.

I have just been painfully dumped by my long-term girlfriend, but she wants us to stay friends. Is it worth it, or should I abandon her completely?

The only sensible advice I have ever heard on this subject came from a friend of mine who works on a submarine. As he so wisely put it, 'If you stay friends, you'll get to feel the side of her tits at funerals.'

My girlfriend talks dirty to me in bed, which I find very off-putting. How can I ask her to stop without seeming too square?

The best solution is the 'mirror technique'. This involves throwing back every comment at her: thus when she says 'Fuck me with your big cock,' you instantly reply 'Fuck me with your big fanny.' When she says 'Ride me, you stallion,' you say 'Ride me, you mare.' Keep this up for a week or two and she'll soon be quieter than Kenny Dalglish.

My pal swears that cunnilingus is better if you suck on a lemon beforehand. Apart from changing the flavour, how can this help?

Taking a hit on a citrus fruit before going down on a woman has nothing to do with making her taste fresher. In fact, it's a method designed to heighten *her* pleasure, not yours, as the sharp acids in the fruit will cause your tastebuds to enlarge, giving your tongue a rough surface which will excite her clitoris more easily. Oh, and a word of advice: limes taste nicer.

Is it safe to have sex during my lover's period?

If you mean 'safe' from a contraceptive point of view, then yes, because it's *extremely* rare for a woman to ovulate during her period. If you're wondering whether it's safe from a physical point of view, then the answer is also yes — the blood that emerges during her period amounts to only a couple of spoonfuls, and it comes from way up in the womb so you're not going to cause any additional bleeding if you thrust too hard. The only real problem with sex when the Gunners are at home is a dry cleaning one, and even then you should be smiling so long as you avoid the first two days of her period, when the flow is heaviest.

How many times is it normal to make love a week?

Stats for this sort of thing are notoriously unreliable, mainly because men tell outrageous lies about their virility, but the latest poll of UK averages for the 16–35 age group works out like this: couples who are married or living together manage it about 135 times a year (roughly 2.5 a week); couples who are going steady but live apart come in at 110 (just over twice a week); single women say they do it 27 times a year (once a fortnight); and — amazingly, given that last figure — single men claim to get lucky 89 times a year (about once every three days.) Liars.

Can a man fake an orgasm?

If you come inside a woman, she's unlikely to be able to feel your semen hitting her vaginal walls. But she may well wonder why there's nothing dribbling out later, so if you can't climax and don't want to hurt her feelings, just whip it out and pretend to come into some tissues.

What's the best music to make love to?

Some people prefer classical stuff like Ravel's *Bolero*, others go for the soothing tones of Marvin Gaye or Barry White. But, as it's entirely a personal decision, I daresay some chaps can only get their rocks off when there's a brass band on the stereo. As for myself, I warmly recommend live albums. If only because you get applause every three minutes.

Is it possible to break your penis?

Although the penis does not contain a bone, (at least not unless Jennifer Aniston is on the telly), it can indeed be snapped. One London urologist estimates that this happens to around 200 British men every year, usually when the woman is on top during sex and bends backwards suddenly. The severe and painful damage to muscle tissue can be cured with minor surgery and a splint, but the long-term damage tends to be of a more psychological nature.

189

No matter how much I turn her on with foreplay, my girlfriend's pussy stays tight and dry. What am I doing wrong?

It may be that she's suffering from a complaint called vaginismus, which is a spasm of the vagina usually caused by a mental trauma earlier in life, such as a rape, an abortion or a painful pregnancy. Women on anti-depressants such as Prozac can also go off sex, and they'll find it equally difficult to get aroused. The only way forward here is for her to see a psychotherapist and work through the causes of her problem, and when she's finally ready to make love again, you should take things exceptionally slo-o-ow and gentle. Above all, while she's undergoing treatment, don't push her to have sex. You have to be patient and play the long game, or things will only get worse.

What's the best way to guarantee that a woman stays faithful?

As they used to advise young men getting married in Yorkshire, 'Keep her well-shagged and poorly shod, and she'll not wander far.'

A SHORT WORD AT THE END...

The casual observer might assume from reading this book that performance in bed is the be-all and end-all of a happy sexual relationship. It isn't, of course. Outside of one night stands, sex is most often an extension of friendship, and the great majority of women would prefer to share their bed with someone who was funny, sweet and kind, rather than a caddish if capable Don Juan. Although this undoubtedly has some drawbacks (and I'm thinking here, in particular, of the habit girls have of giving our penises a 'cute' pet name), it's a reality you too should see as welcome. After all, while it's great to have fantastic, Olympic-gymnastic-medal-winning sex, sometimes you just want to laze around with a companionable partner. Personally, I know I look back with as much fondness on certain slow, affectionate sexual encounters in my past as I do on those ones which had a more frenzied, pornographic quality.

It's also important to note that sex is for everyone[1], even the inept. Anything from stress at work to boredom, from physical unfitness to disability, could impede someone from doing any or all of the stuff we've covered in these pages. And even those of you who are up for every manoeuvre will have to compromise when faced with mood swings or arguments with your partner. My aim has merely been to plant some good ideas in your head. If you try just one tenth of them, you'll be making excellent progress. Of this fraction, too, only some

will work for you, as everyone has different likes and dislikes. The main thing to keep in mind is not what I've told you to do with your fingers or your lips, but with your IMAGINATION. Be open-minded and experimental, don't be bashful about communicating with each other in bed, and you'll probably be inspired to develop your own unique tricks and variations.

If this does happen, then do the world a favour. Write to me c/o HarperCollins, 77–85 Fulham Palace Road, Hammersmith, London W6 8JB with your discoveries. If enough of you put in the hours and come up with the goods, then I'll include them in another volume to help even more lovers gain satisfaction. That I will then put the proceeds towards the purchase of a large, agreeable house in the hills above Antibes should in no way deter you from doing your bit for Britain.

Lastly, I sincerely hope that *Real Sex* helps you to enjoy your love life more. When freed from its attendant anxieties, sex has a wonderful, unifying power that can strengthen the bond of love; it's free; it's good exercise; and it sends people off to work in a good mood, thus resulting in a cheerful, industrious population and a boost to productivity.

So read this book again, and get under that duvet. The recession ends here.

Guy Smith.

---

[1] *Apart from your parents, obviously.*

INDEX